# COLOR US COSMIC

## COLORING BOOK

### Into the Artworld of RAS TERMS

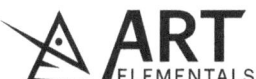

ART
ELEMENTALS

Published by ART Elementals
www.artelementals.com

All Artwork © 2017 by Ras Terms (James Monk)
www.rasterms.com


For permissions and information please write to:

ART Elementals
P.O. Box 1725
Madison, WI 53701
Scott@artelementals.com


All Artwork by: Ras Terms
Project Director: Scott Smith
Layout: Elena Reznikova
        Gabrielle Tesfaye

# ABOUT the ARTIST

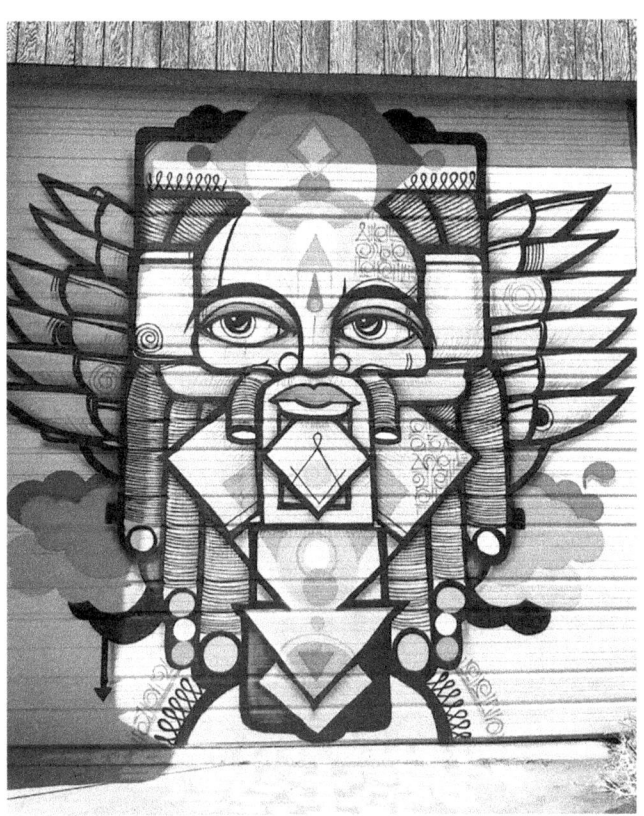

*Mural by Ras Terms. Denver, Colorado.*

Ras Terms, a.k.a. James Monk, was born and raised in Miami, Florida with a Puerto Rican and Columbian background. In addition to living in the Bay Area for the last ten years, he has been traveling throughout the United States, creating art and murals, participating in exhibitions, and experiencing the vastness of life. He began to create art at a very young age, remembering how his mother gave him crayons to color to calm him down in his youth. He eventually started doing graffiti at 11 years old, writing his name everywhere around the streets of Miami.

Still practicing graffiti and street art today, Ras Terms is known as a "letter master" and the "builder of letters." He is also viewed as a spiritual artist with a mastery of a variety of styles. During his early work, he served as a conduit to the creative powers, fusing his letter styles with art and fun, reminding people through visuals to maintain the codes of peace, unity, love, and to have fun. Now older and living in the Bay Area, his work has taken a break from heavily-influenced spirituality and has matured on to more contemporary, abstract styles. He says, "If you ask me about my work, I may say something about African-Indian-alchemy-voodoo, or I may just point out something hilarious." These days, he is greatly inspired by Steve Jobs' quote, "Stay hungry. Stay foolish."

Spreading his mission all over the world, Ras Terms' work can be seen on everything from clothing and stickers, to large scale murals. He embodies his craft entirely while living his life, believing that "the creative force is non-judgmental and the only thing constant and true in life." Today, his contemporary art is recognized on a global scale. He continues to travel and create on a constant basis, collaborating with a broad range of artists and painting the walls of cities around the globe.

Welcome to the artworld of Ras Terms . . .

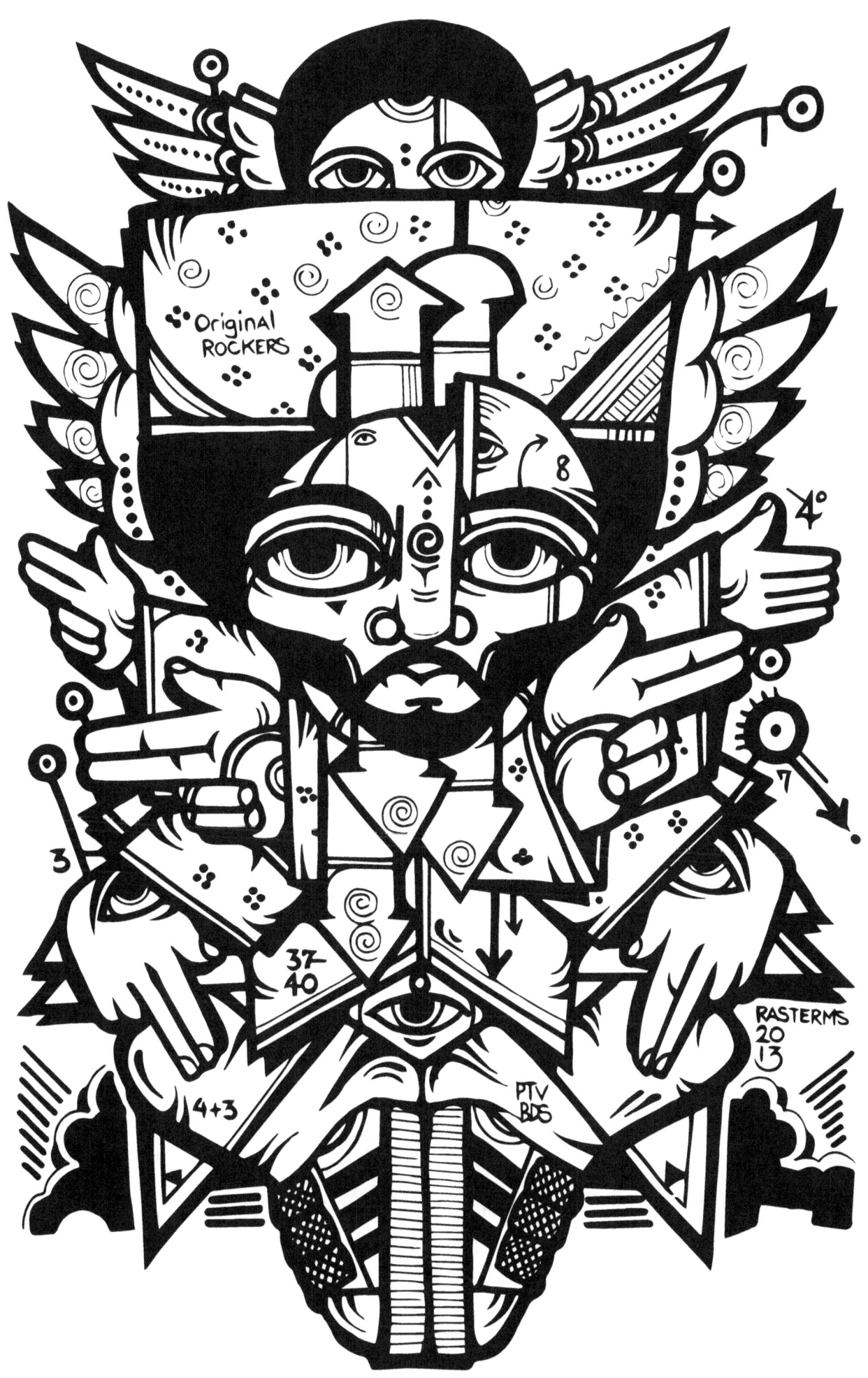

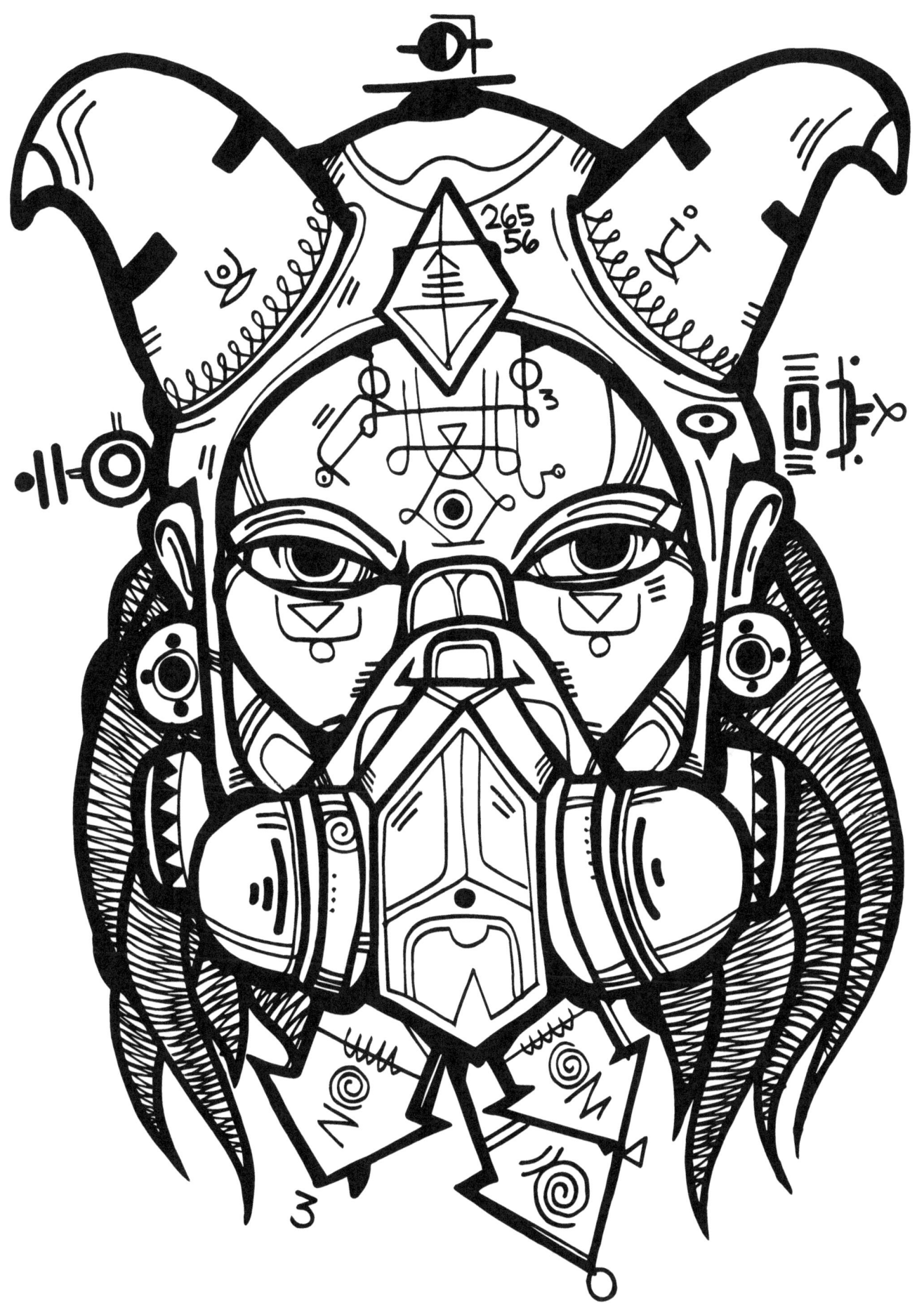

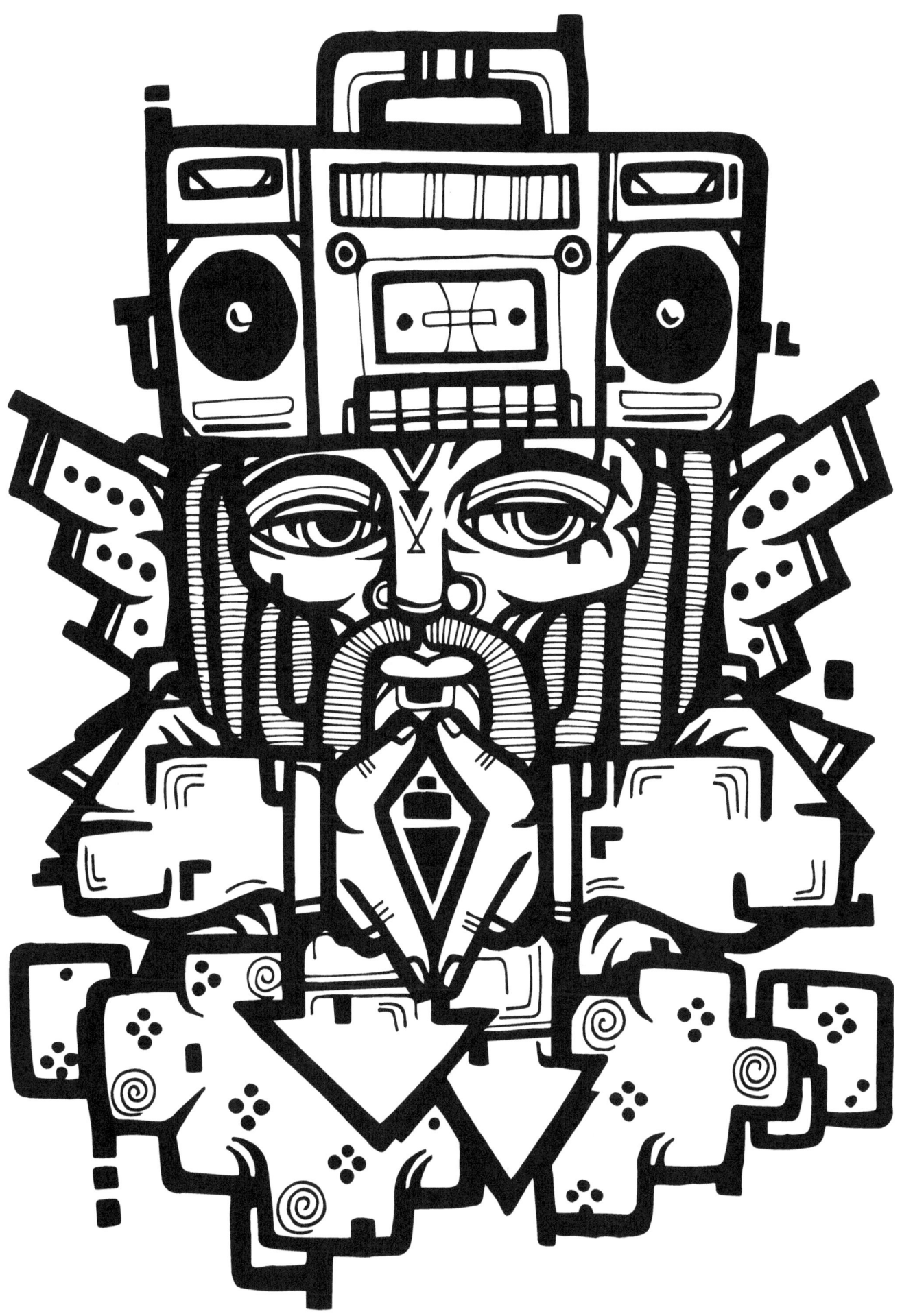

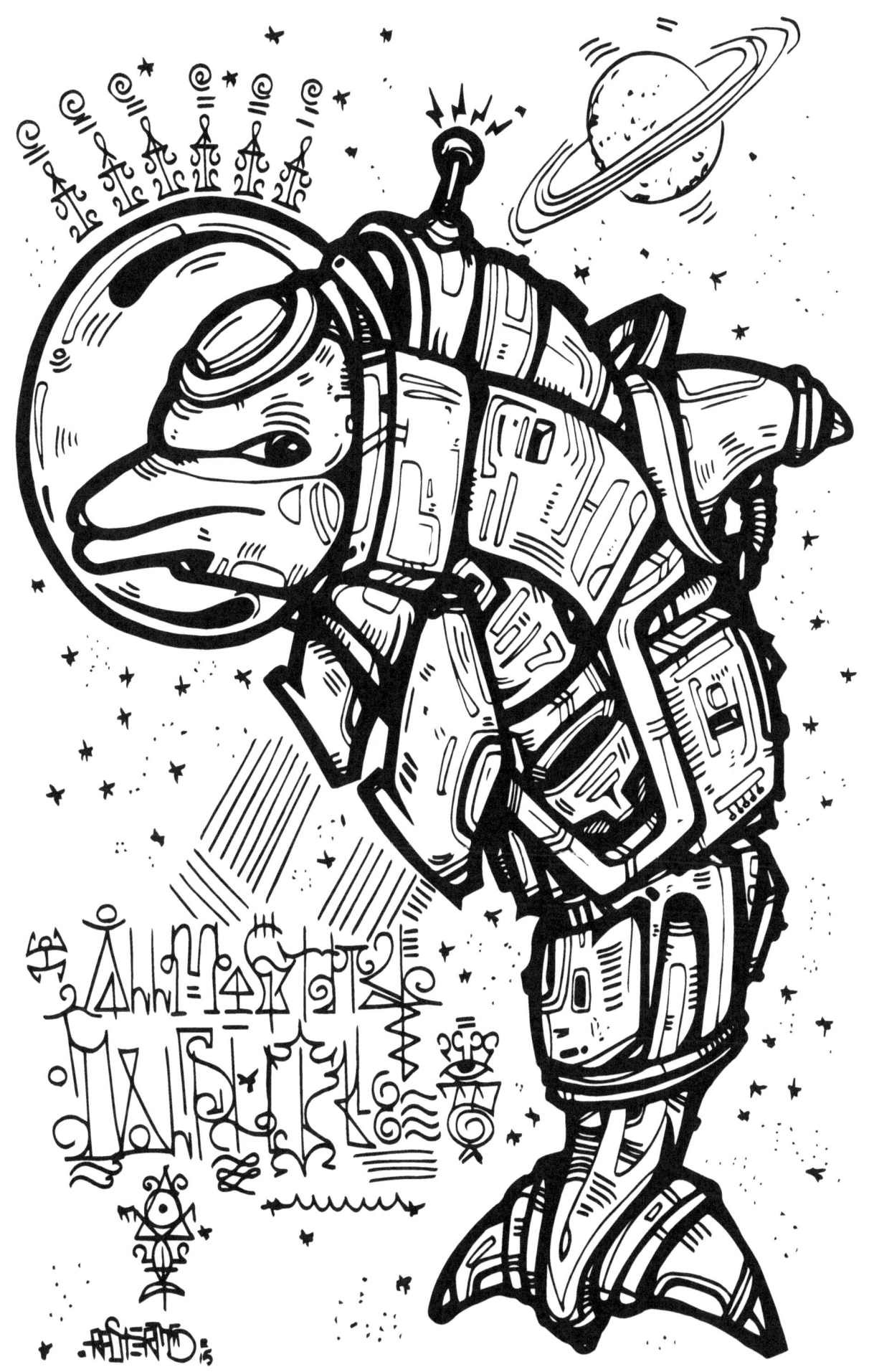

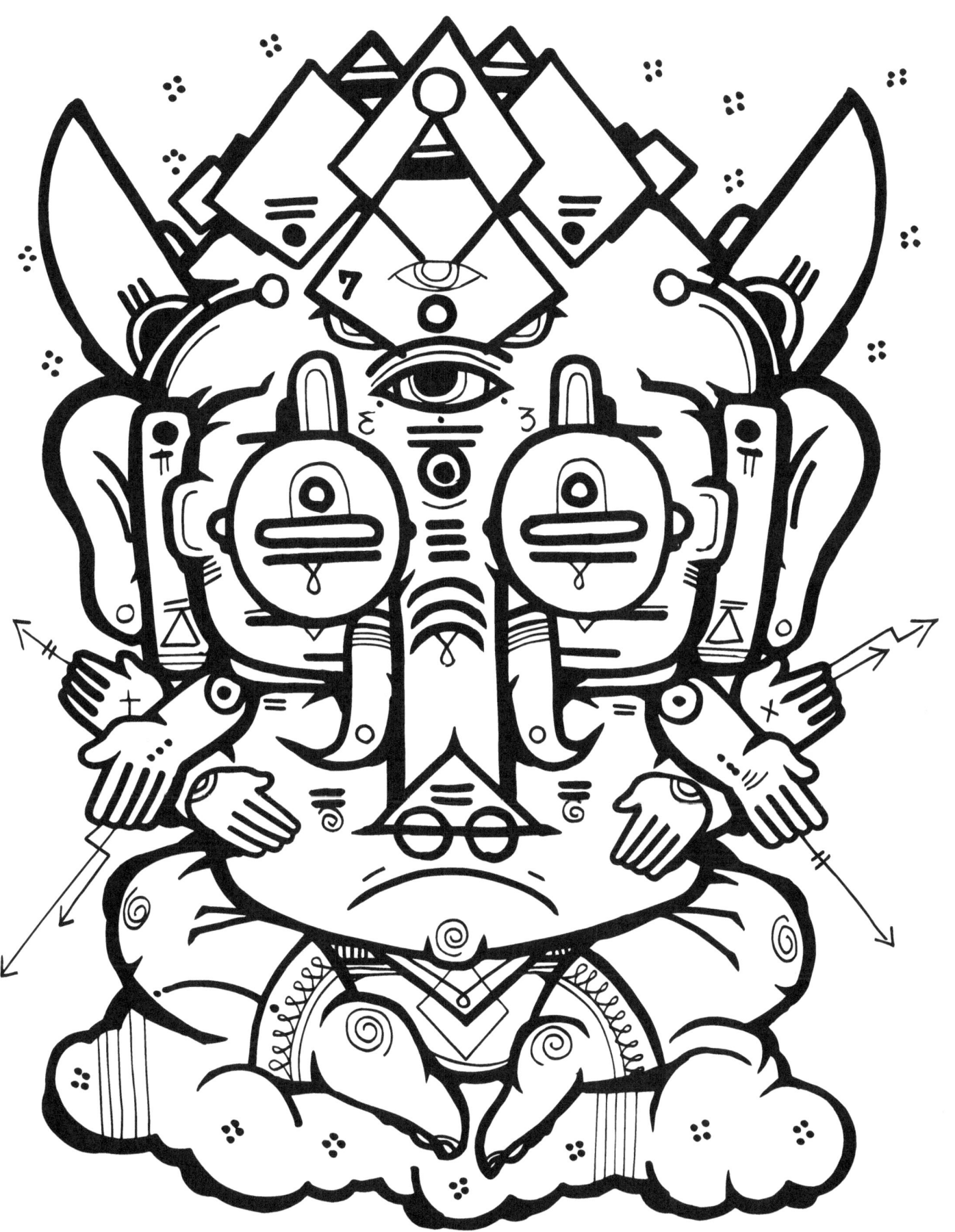

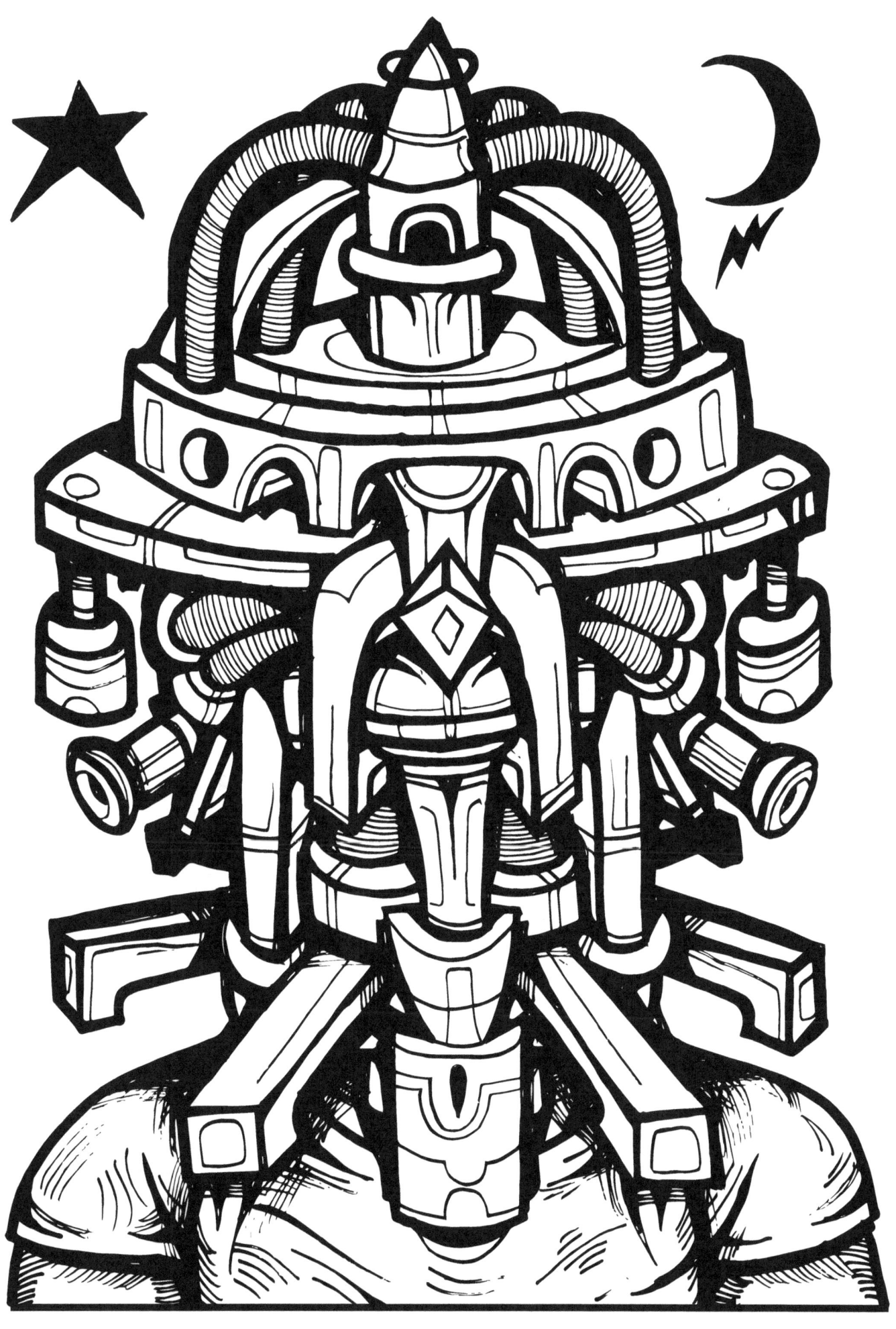

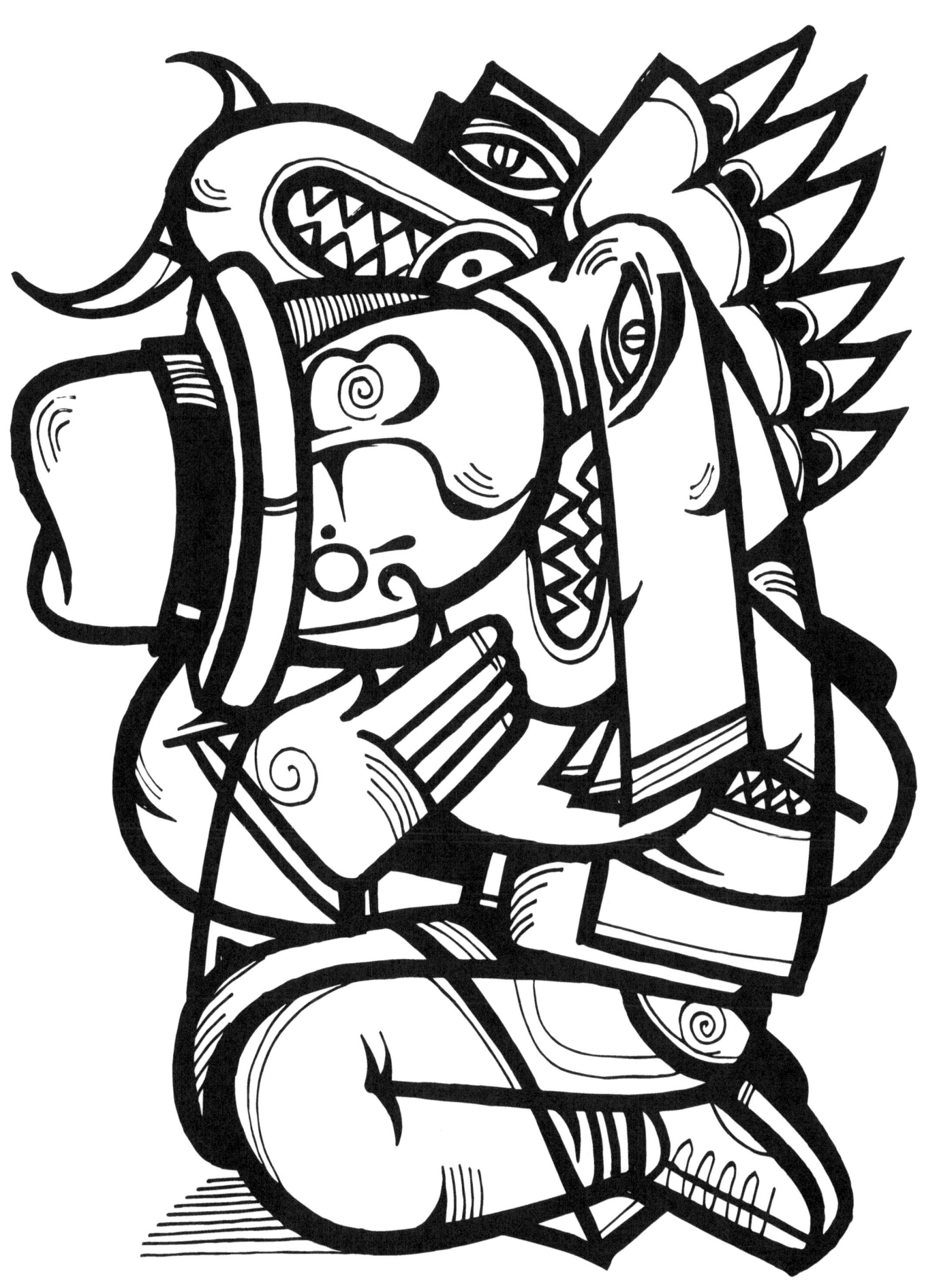

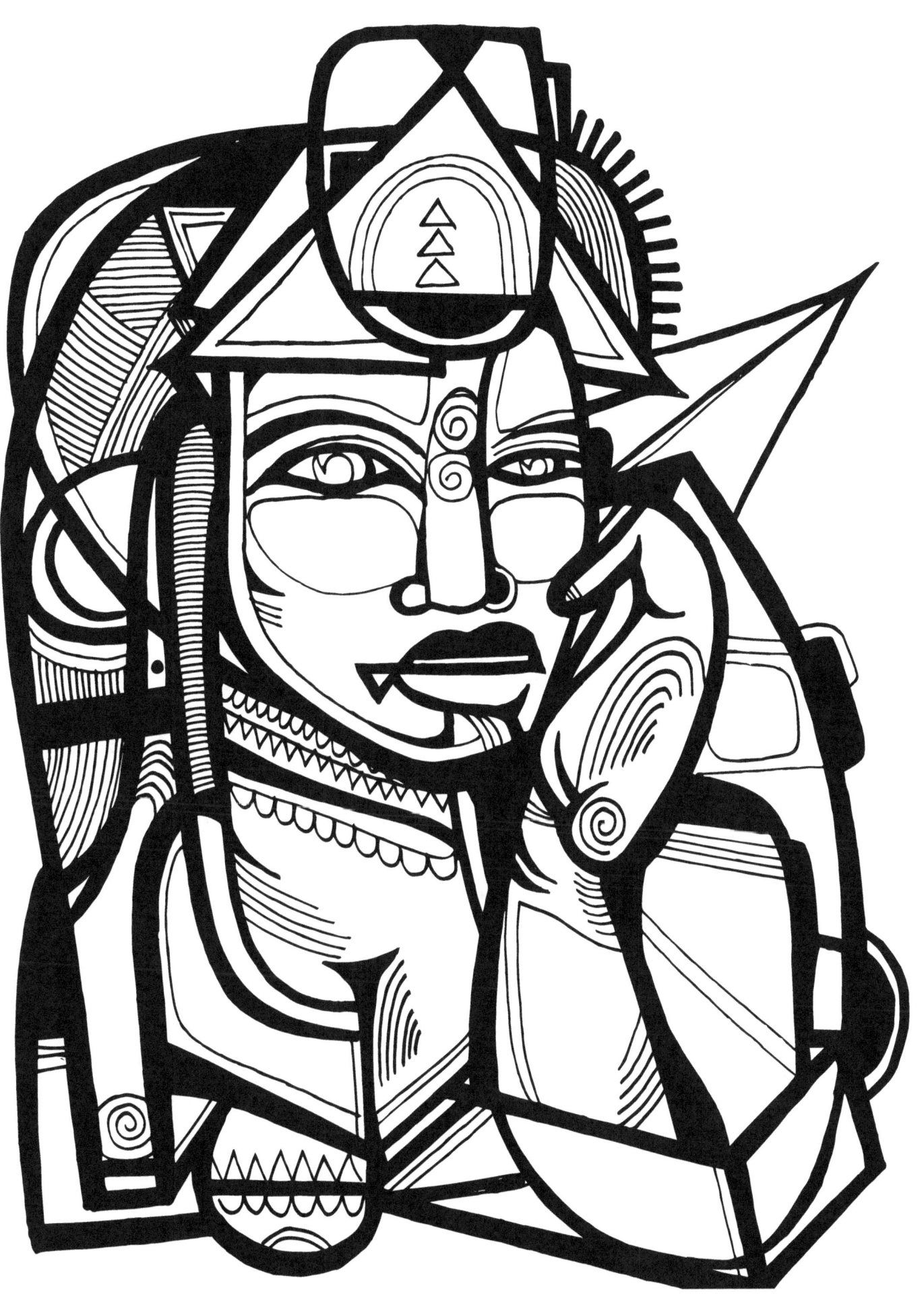

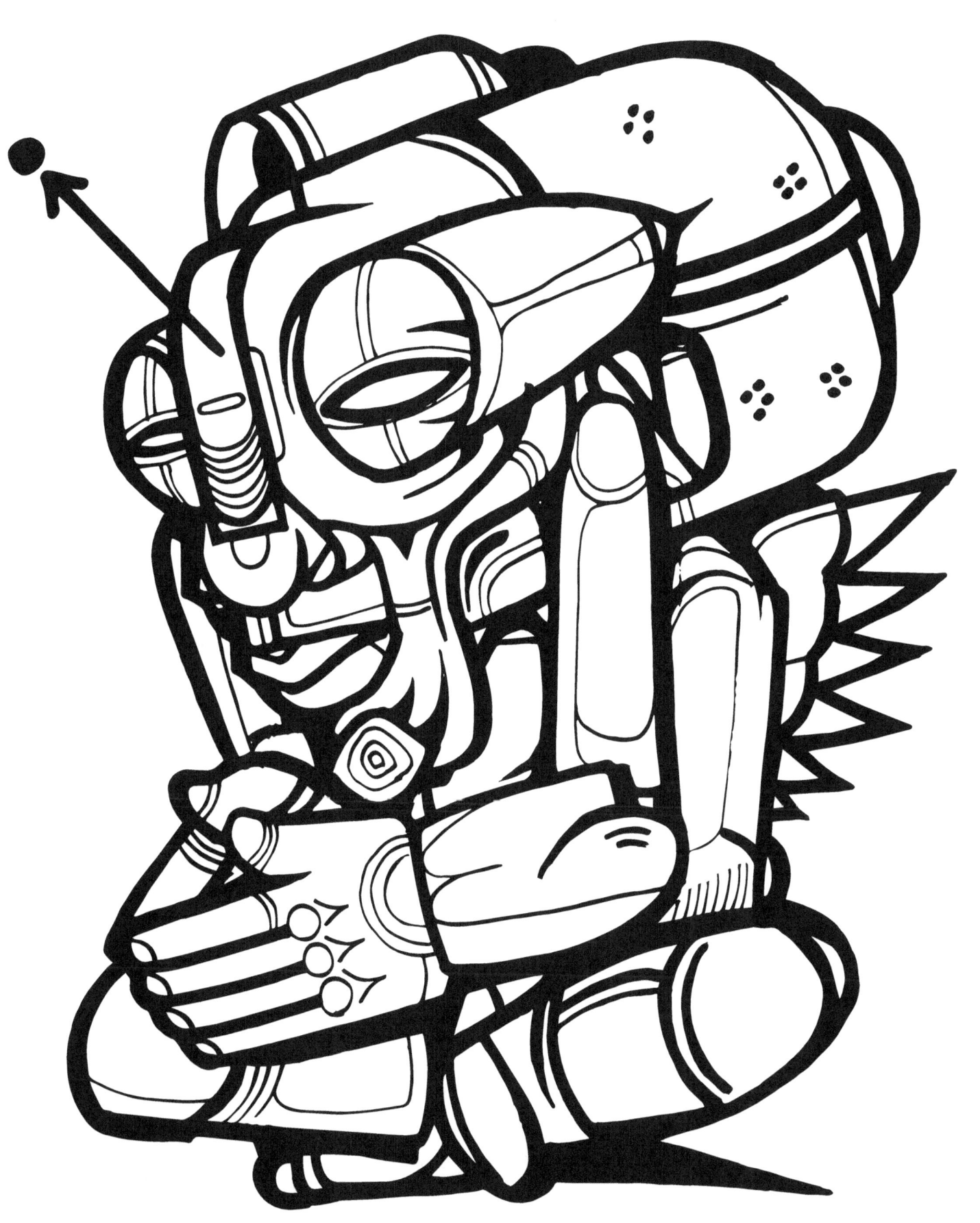

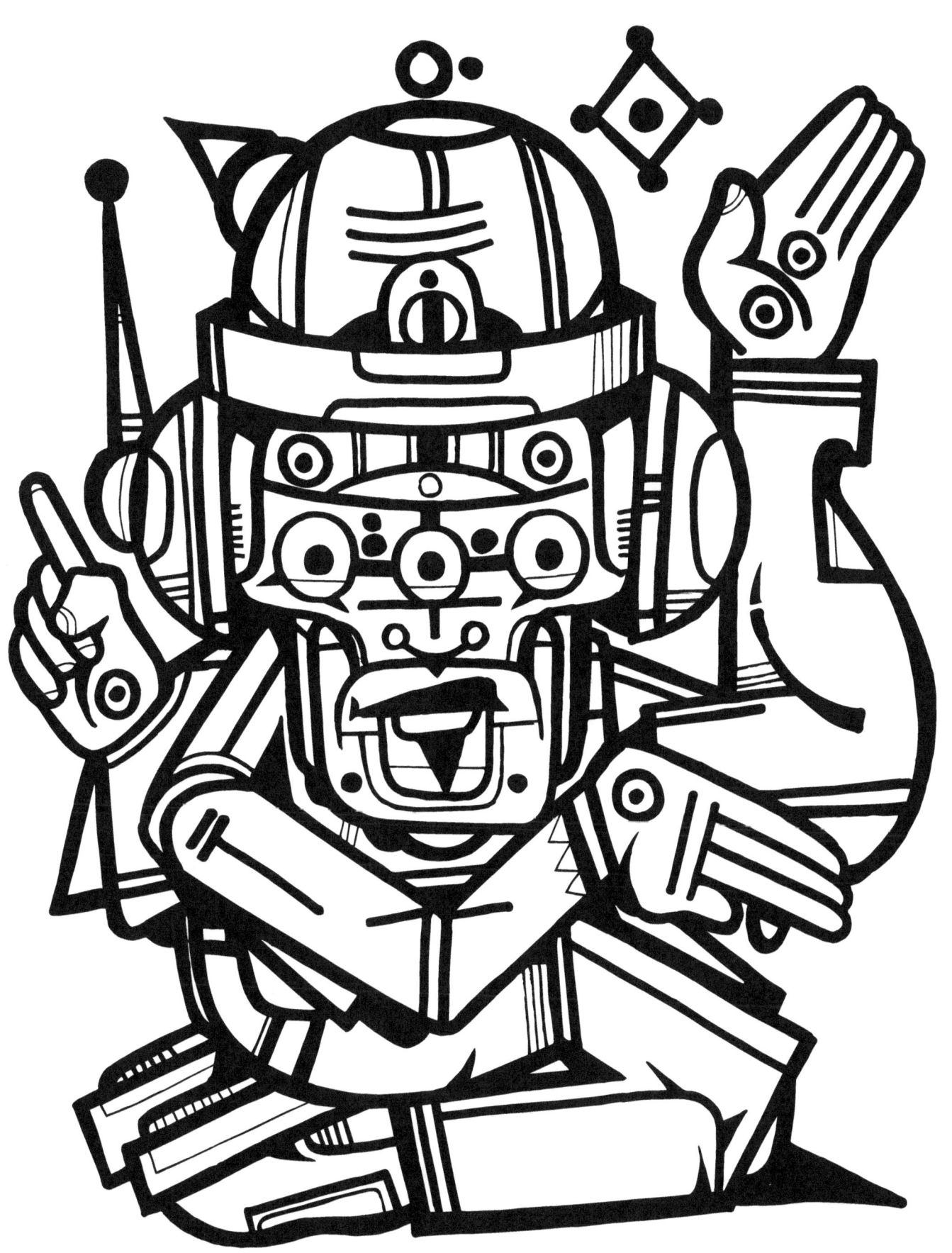

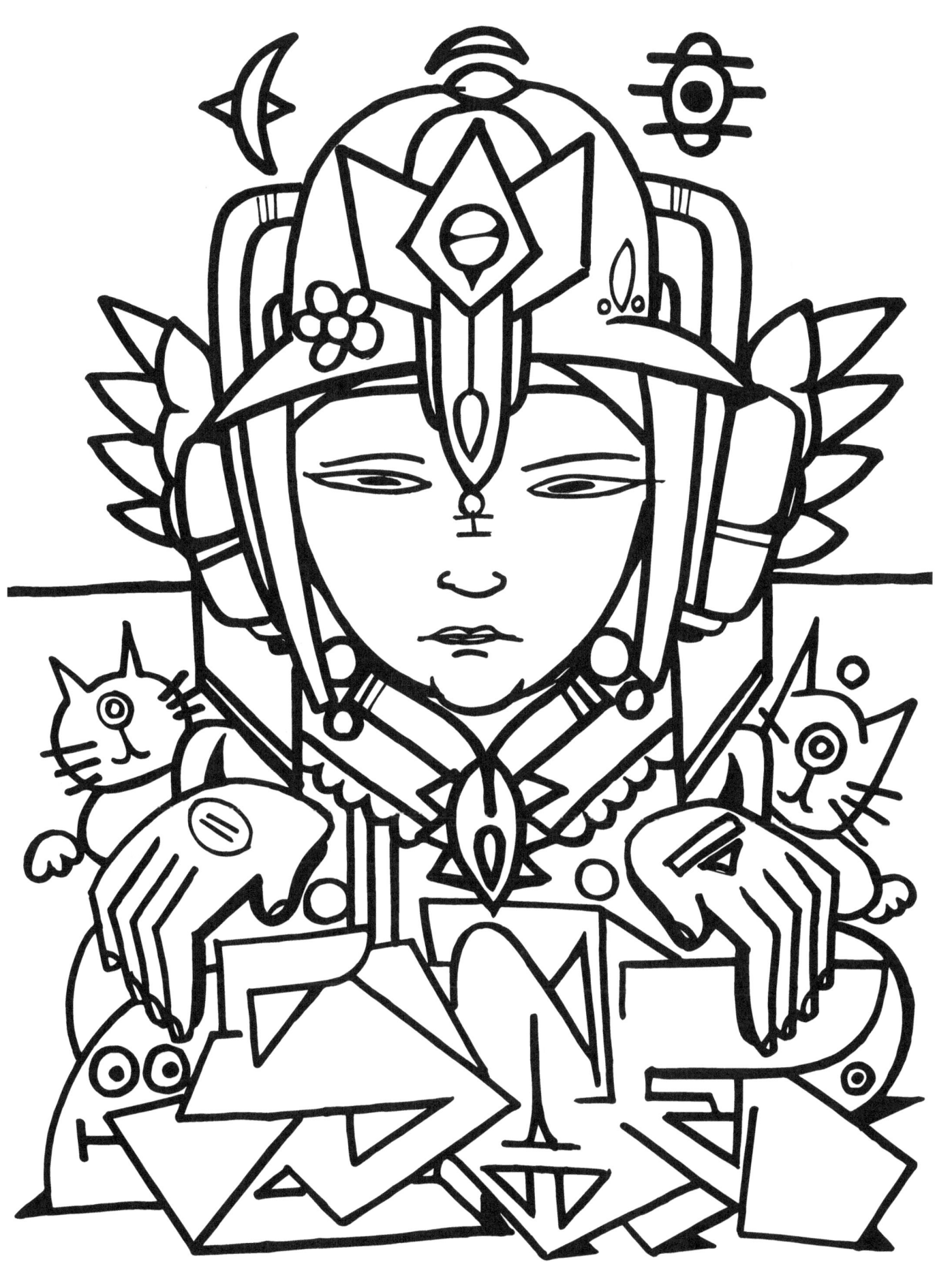

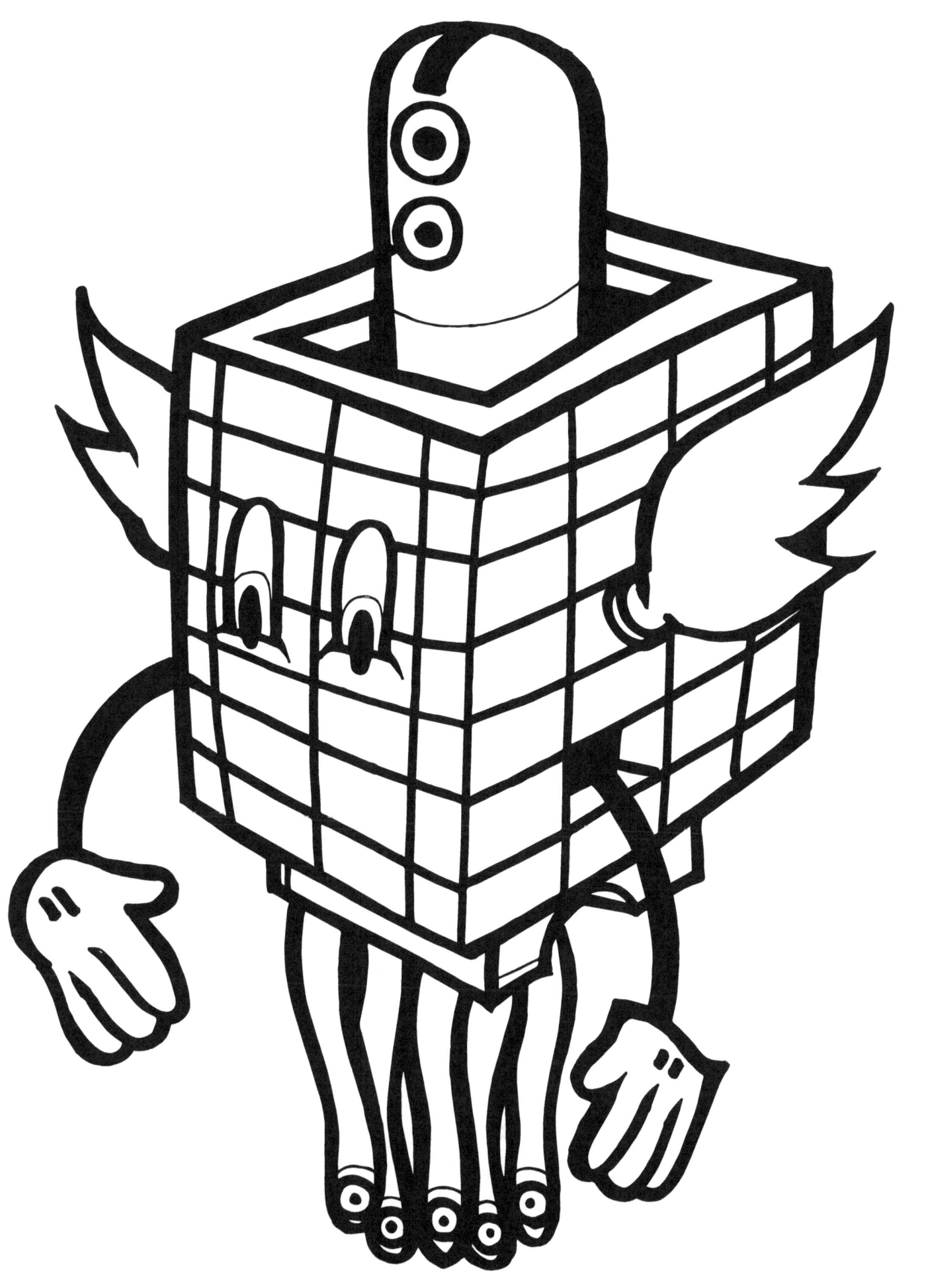

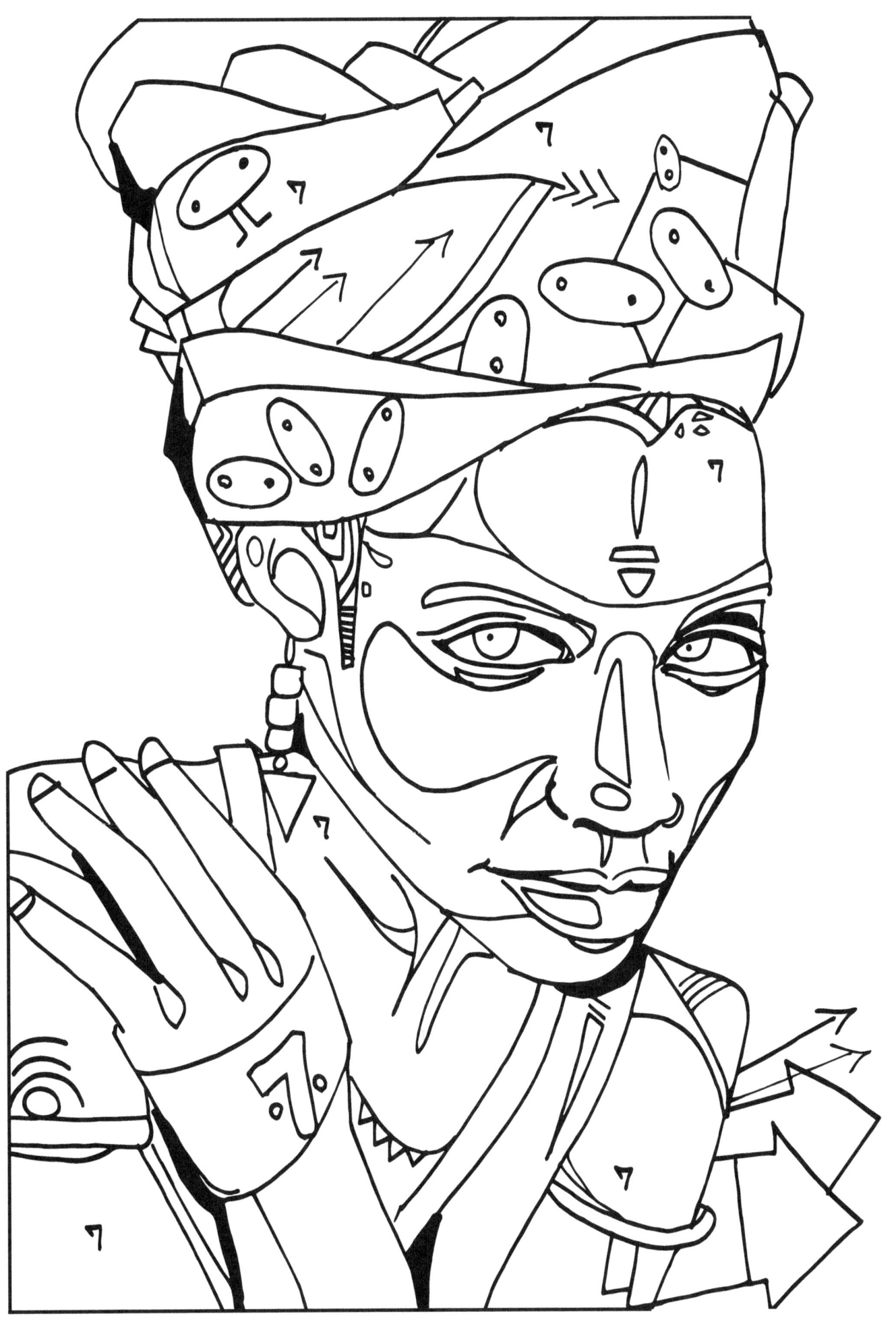

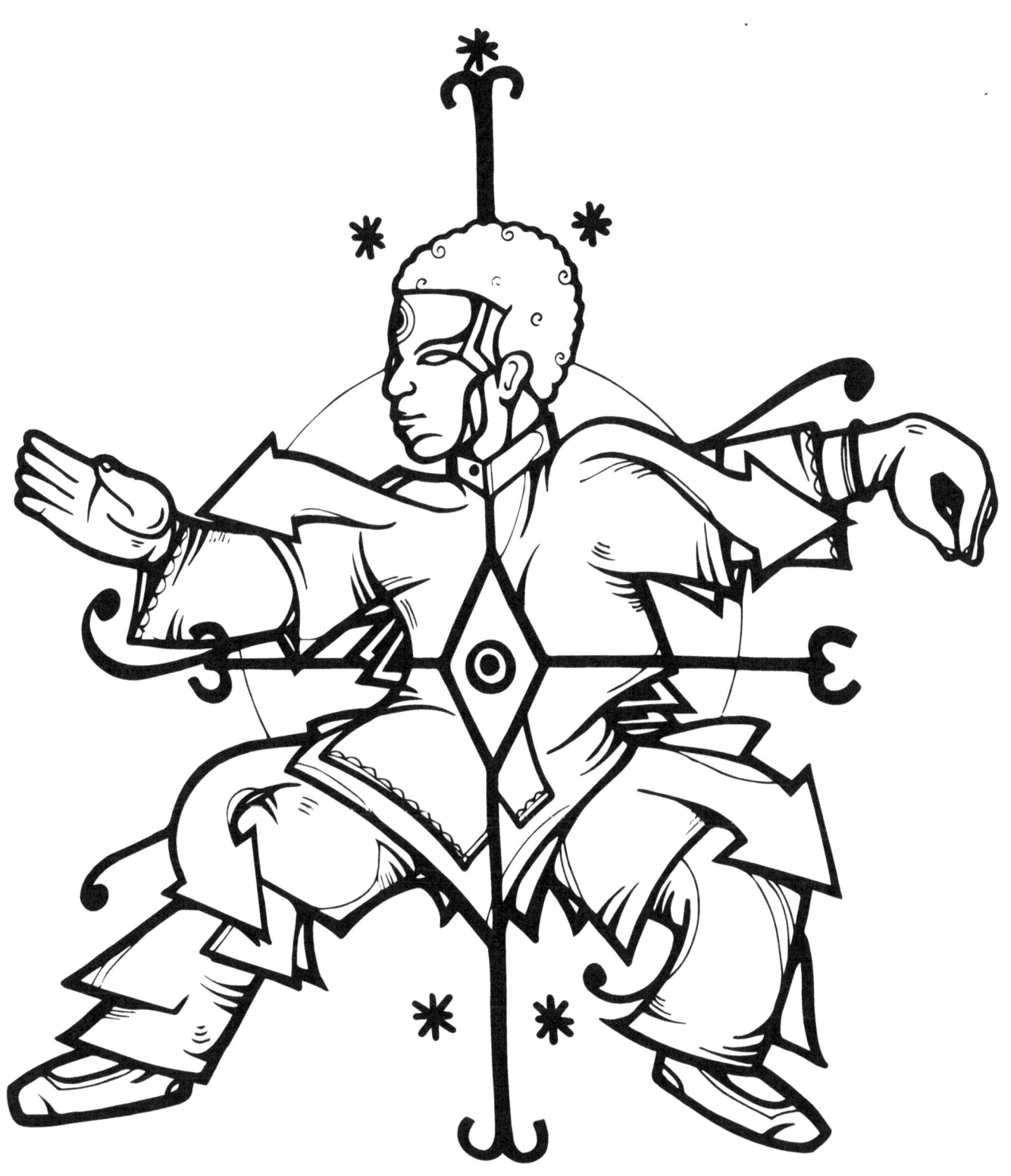

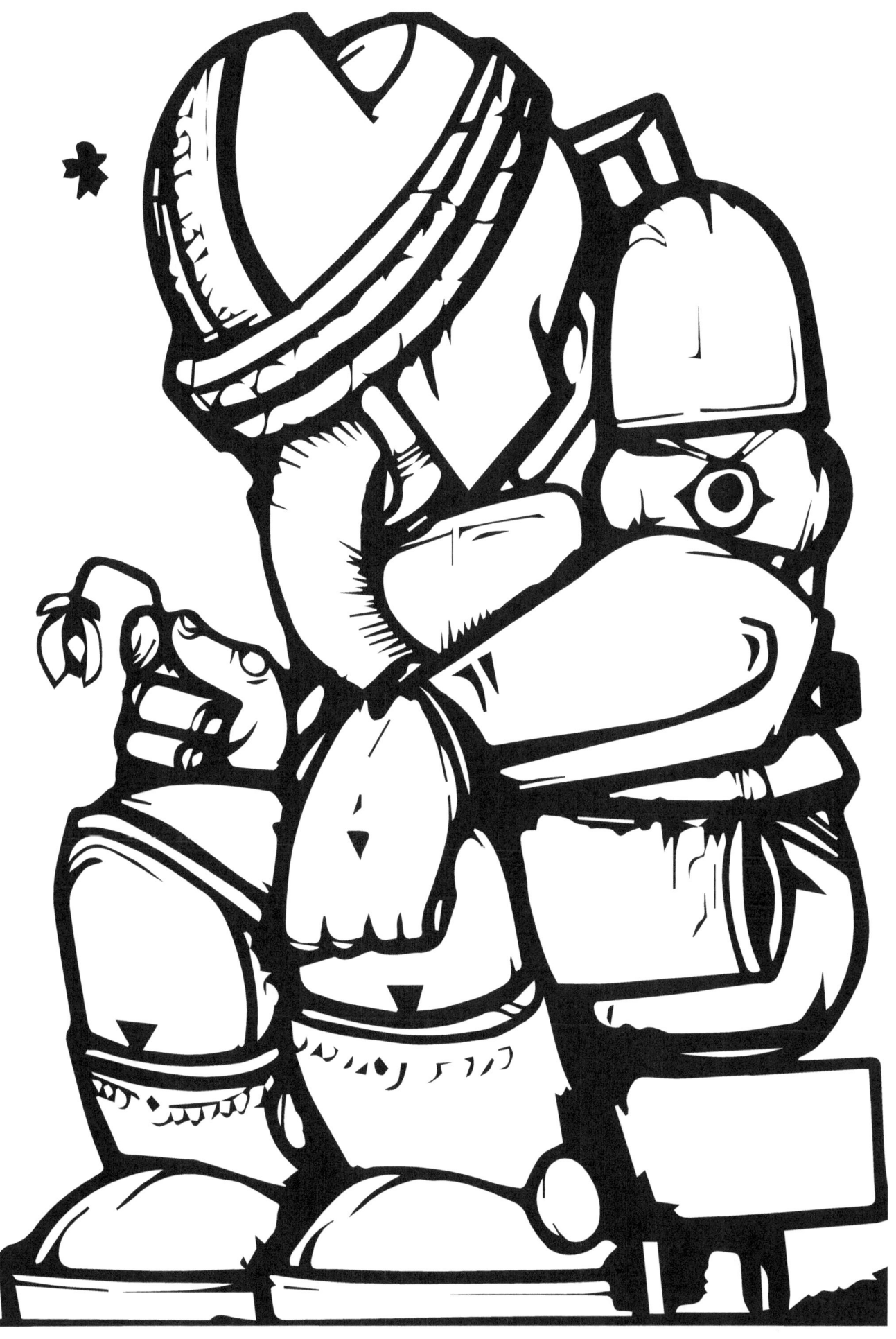

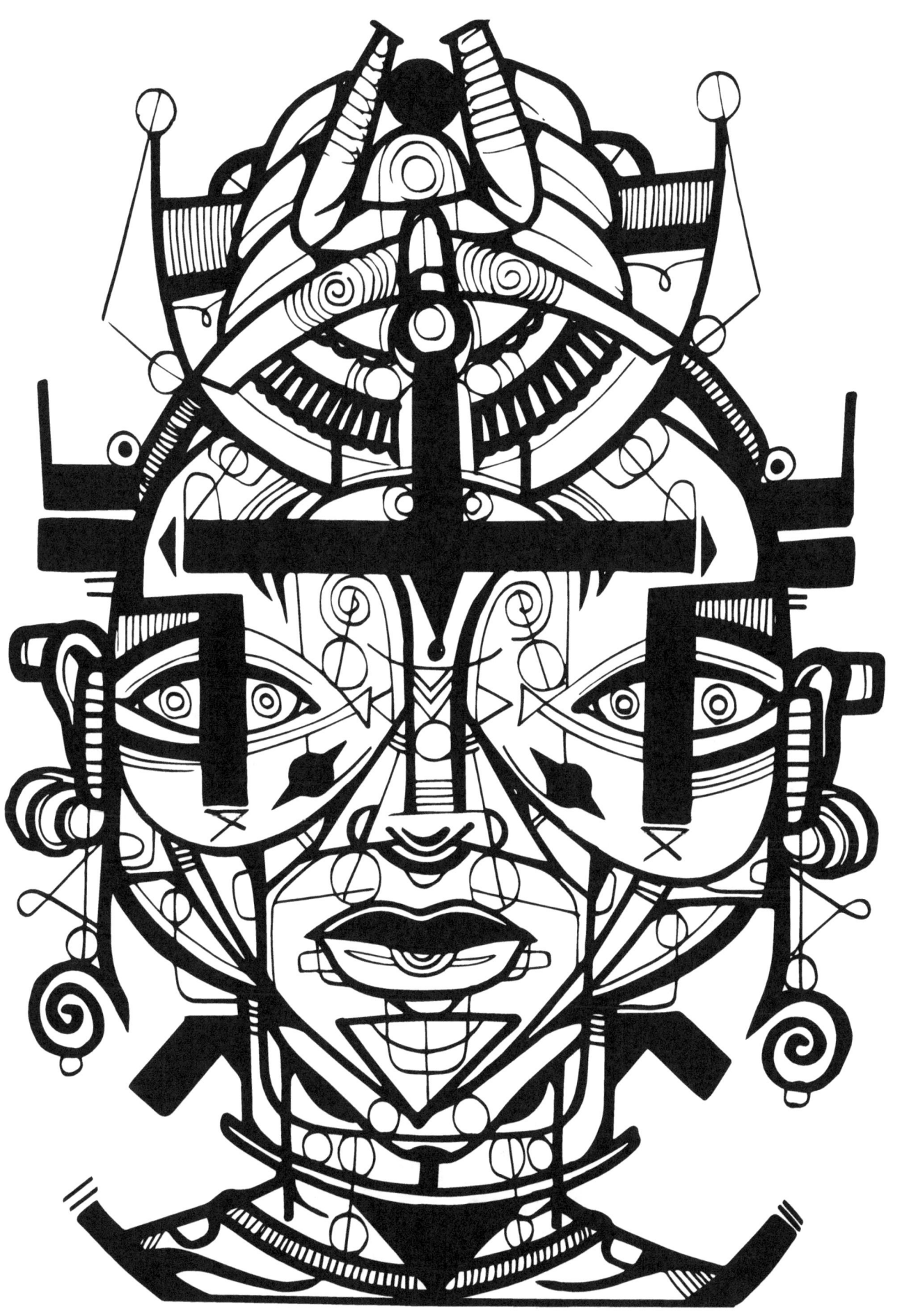

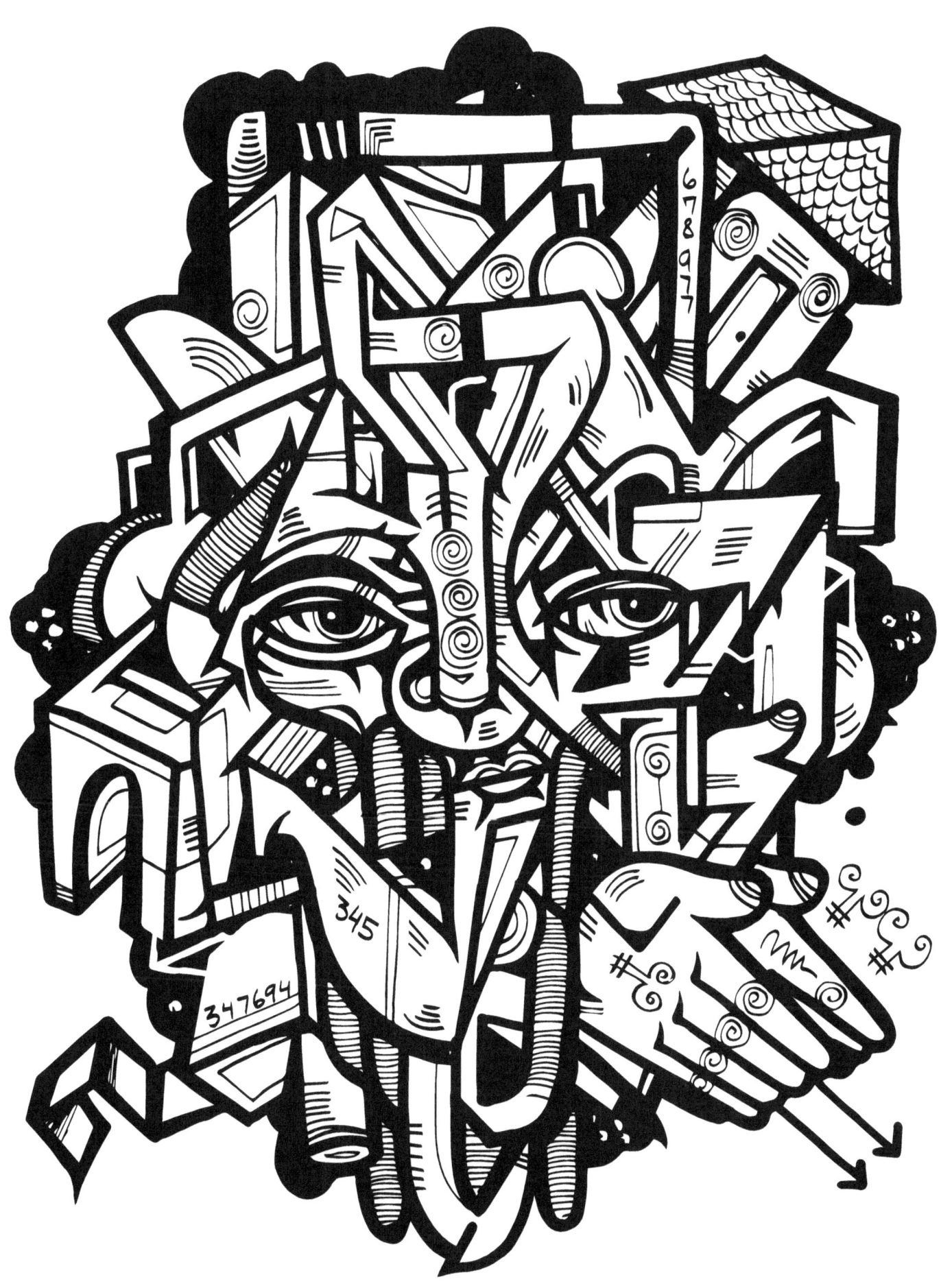

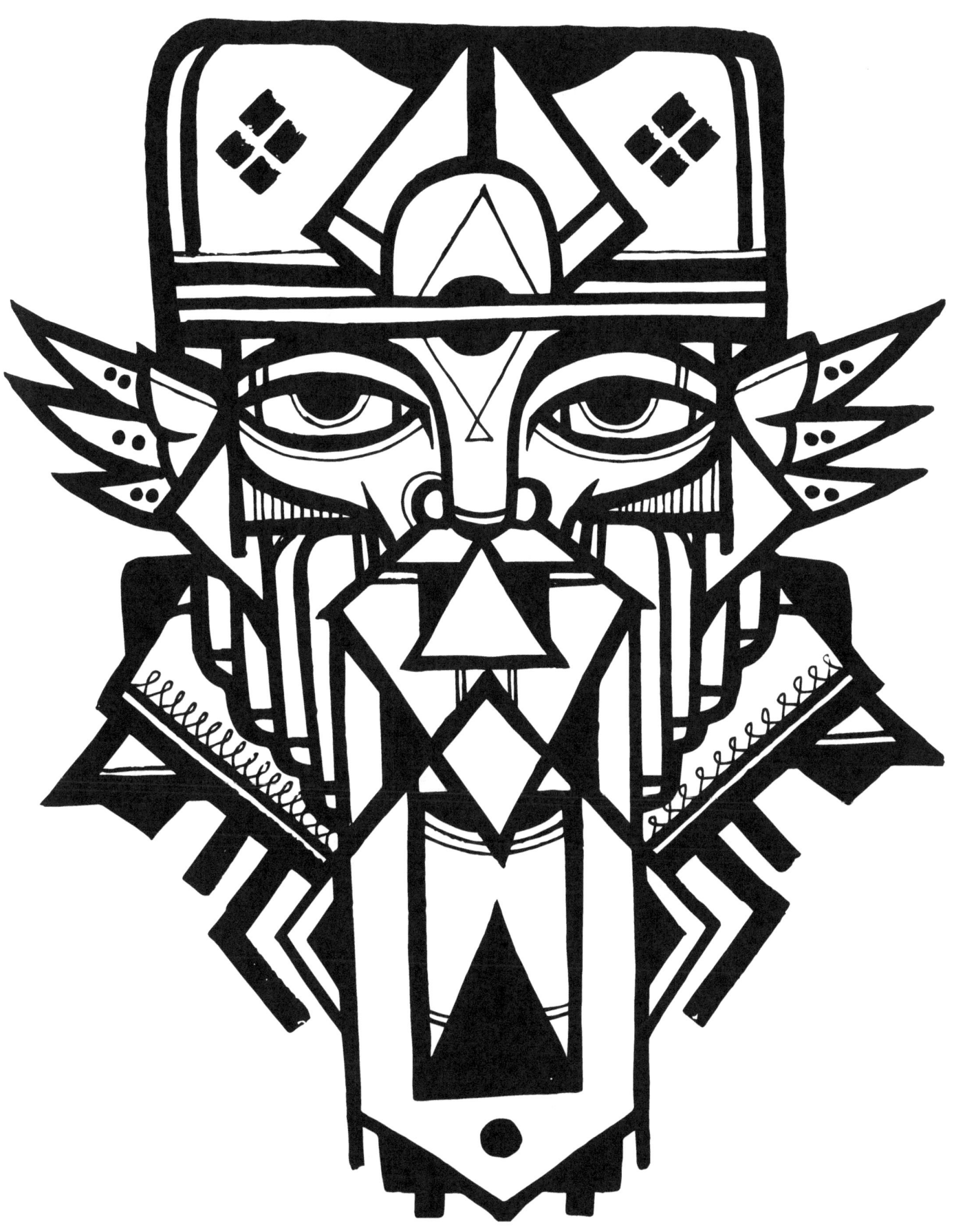

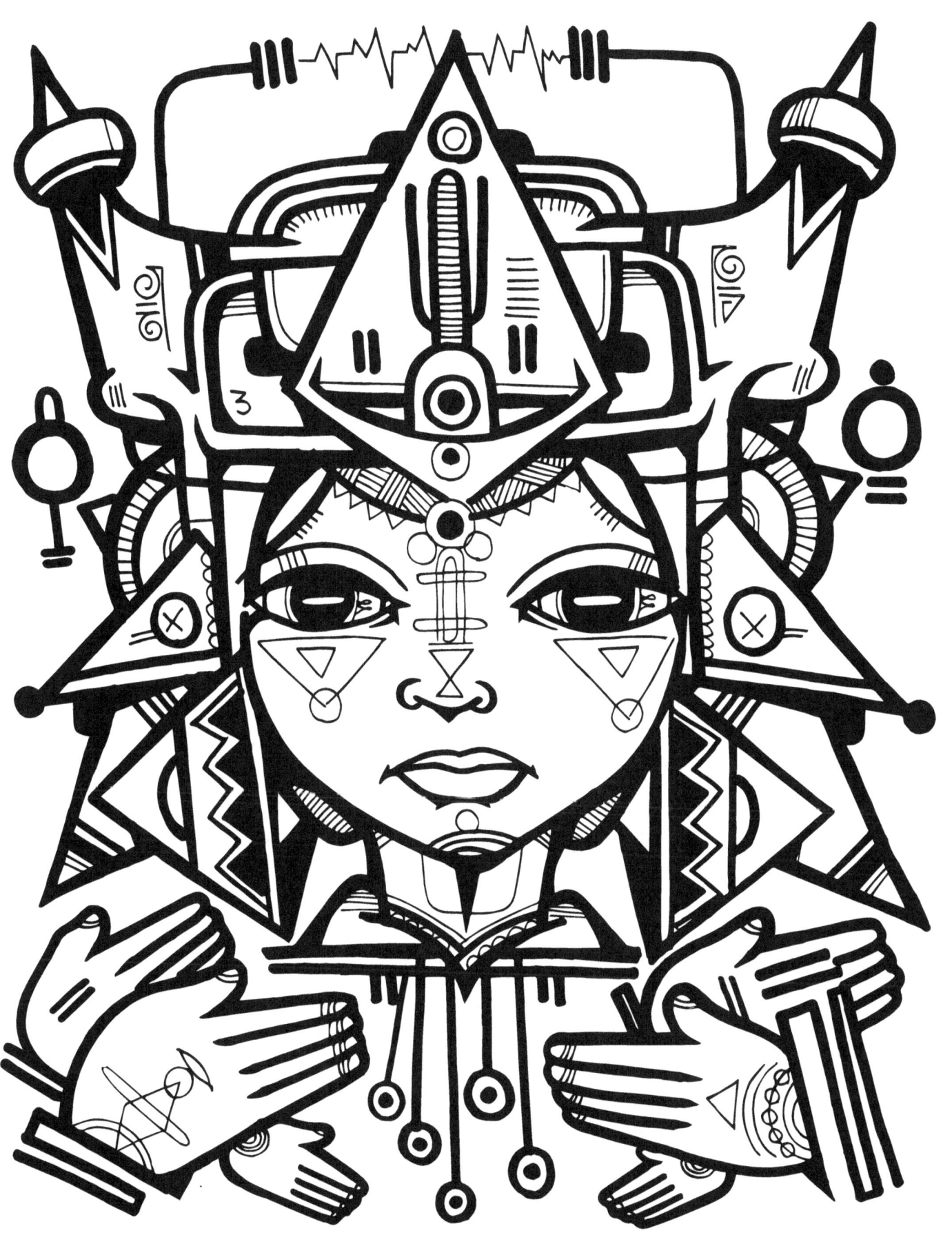

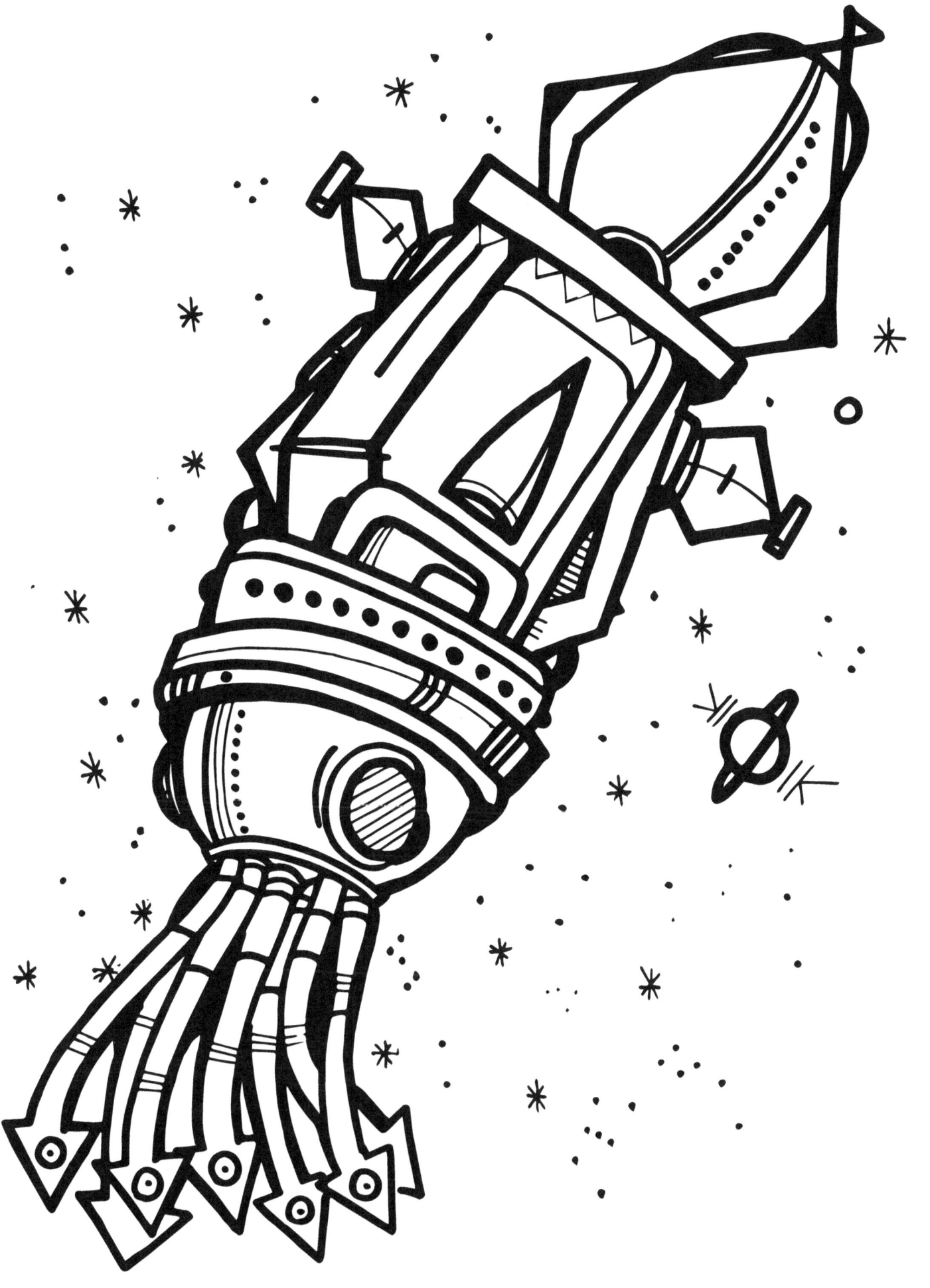

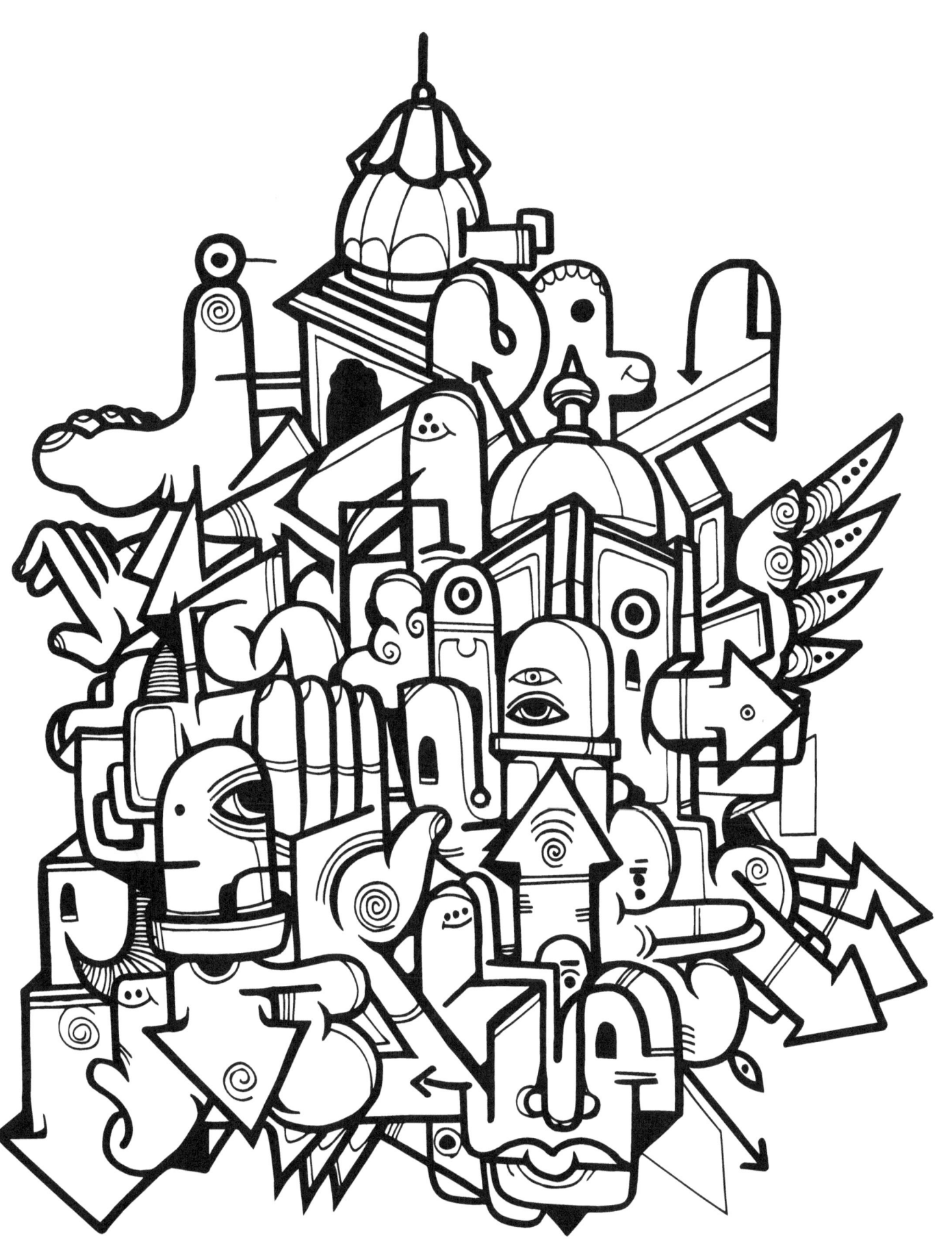

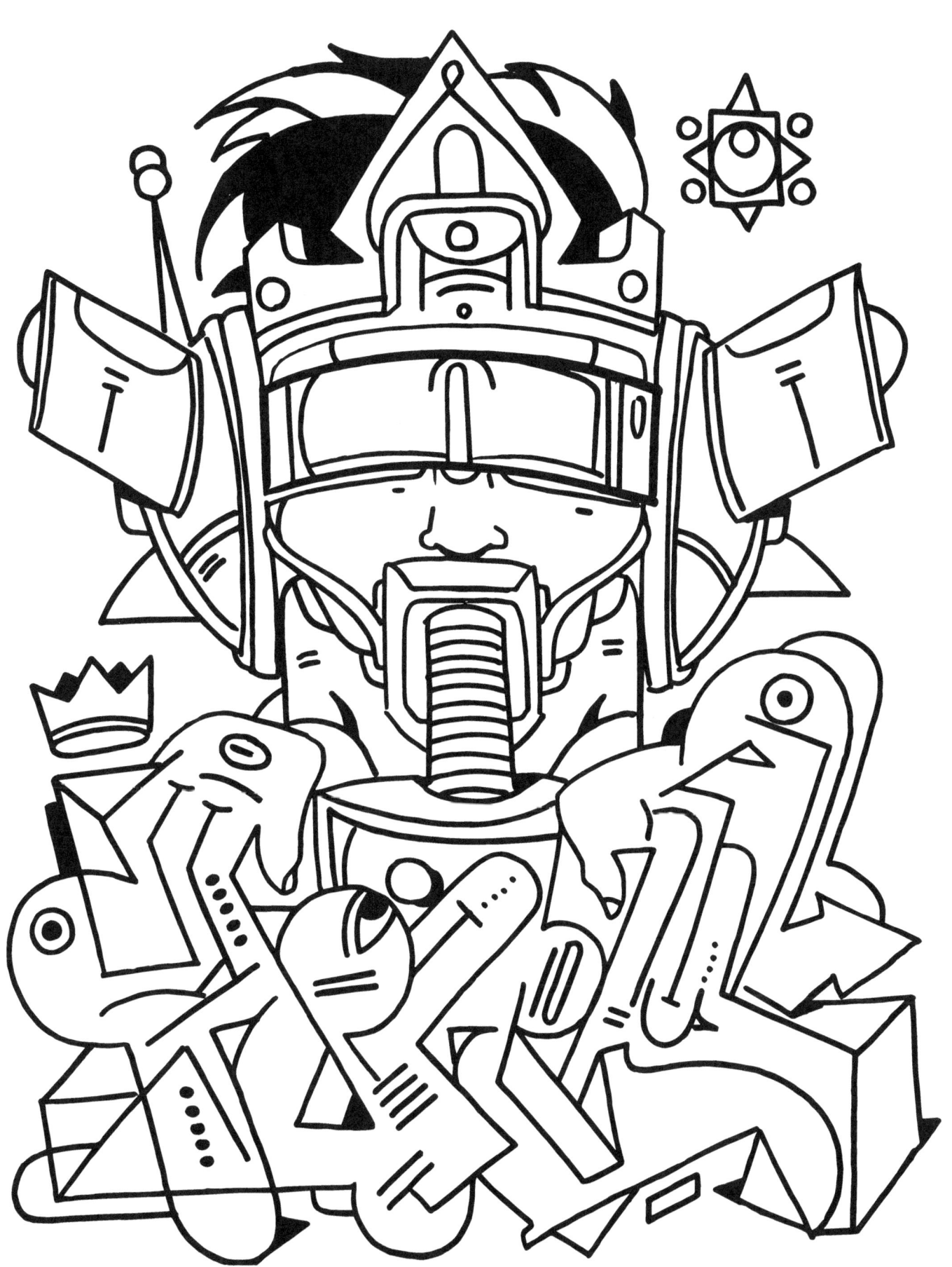

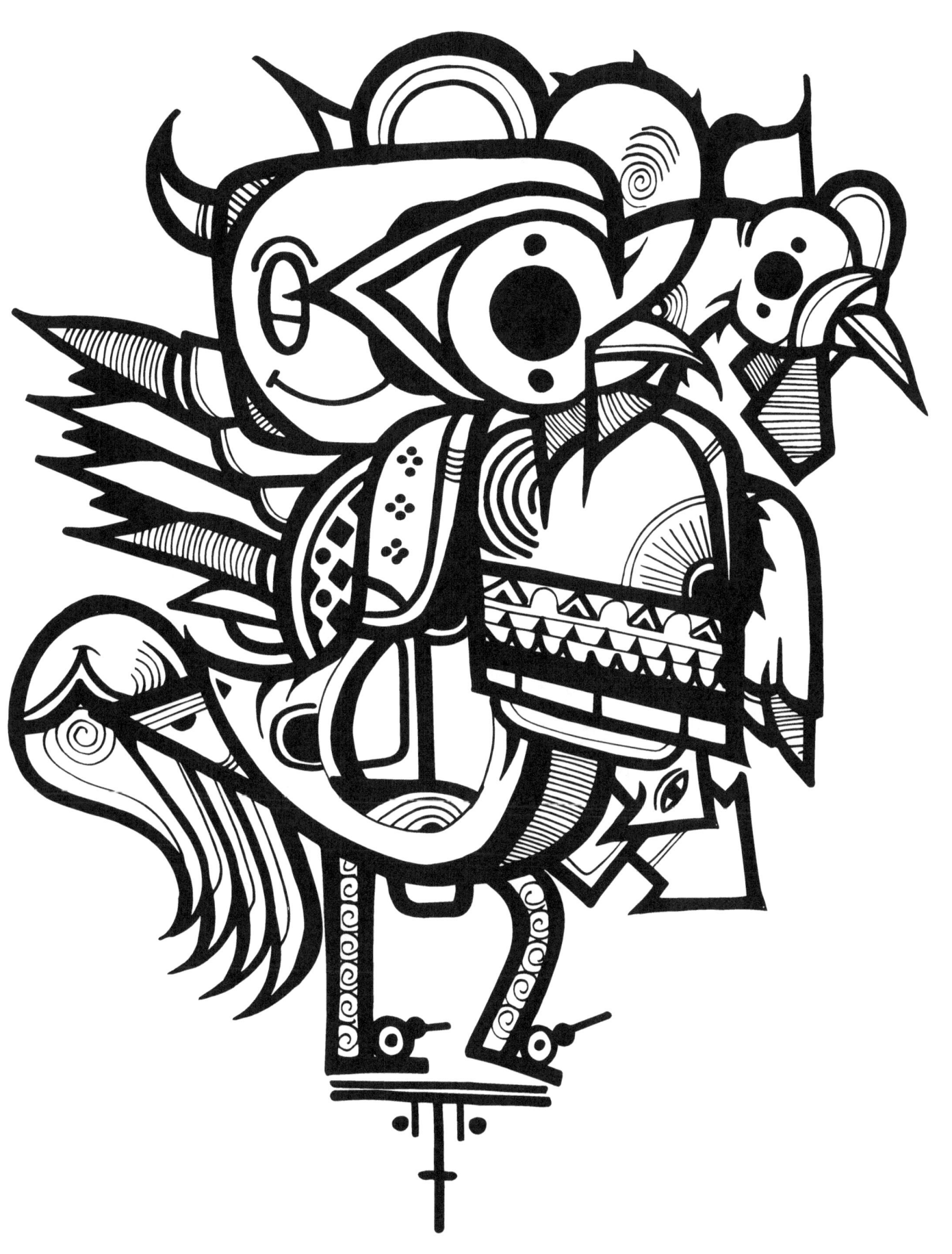

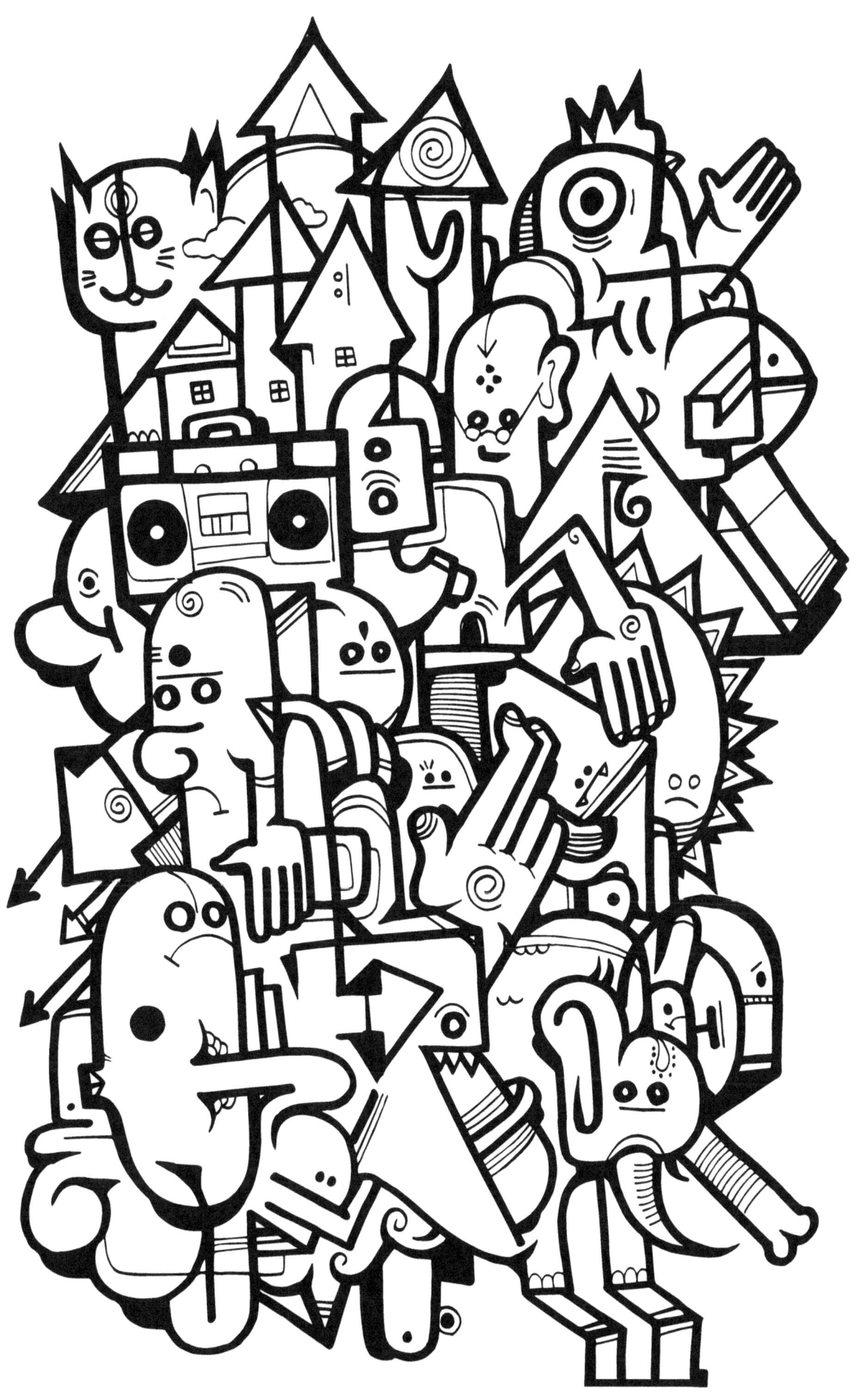

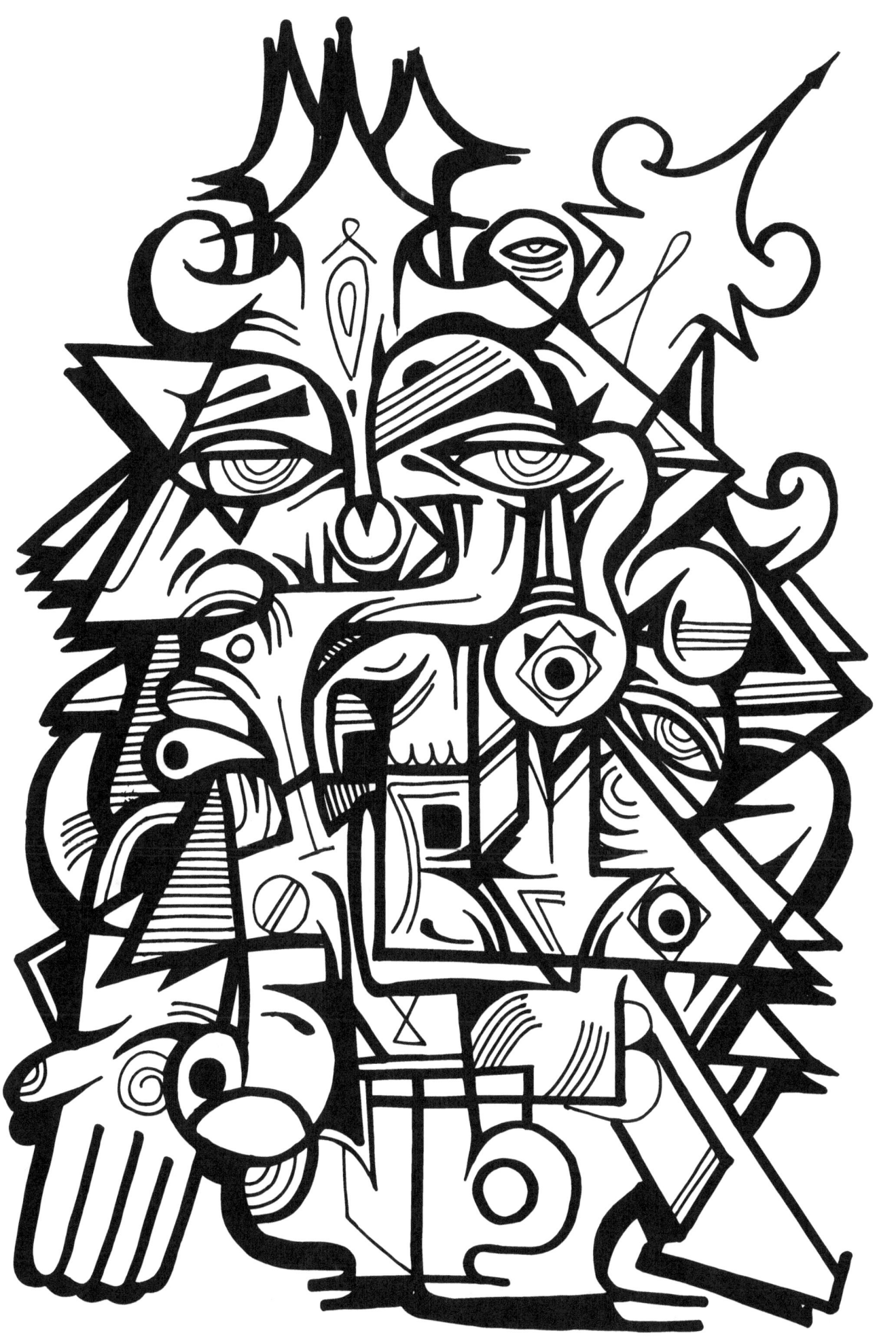

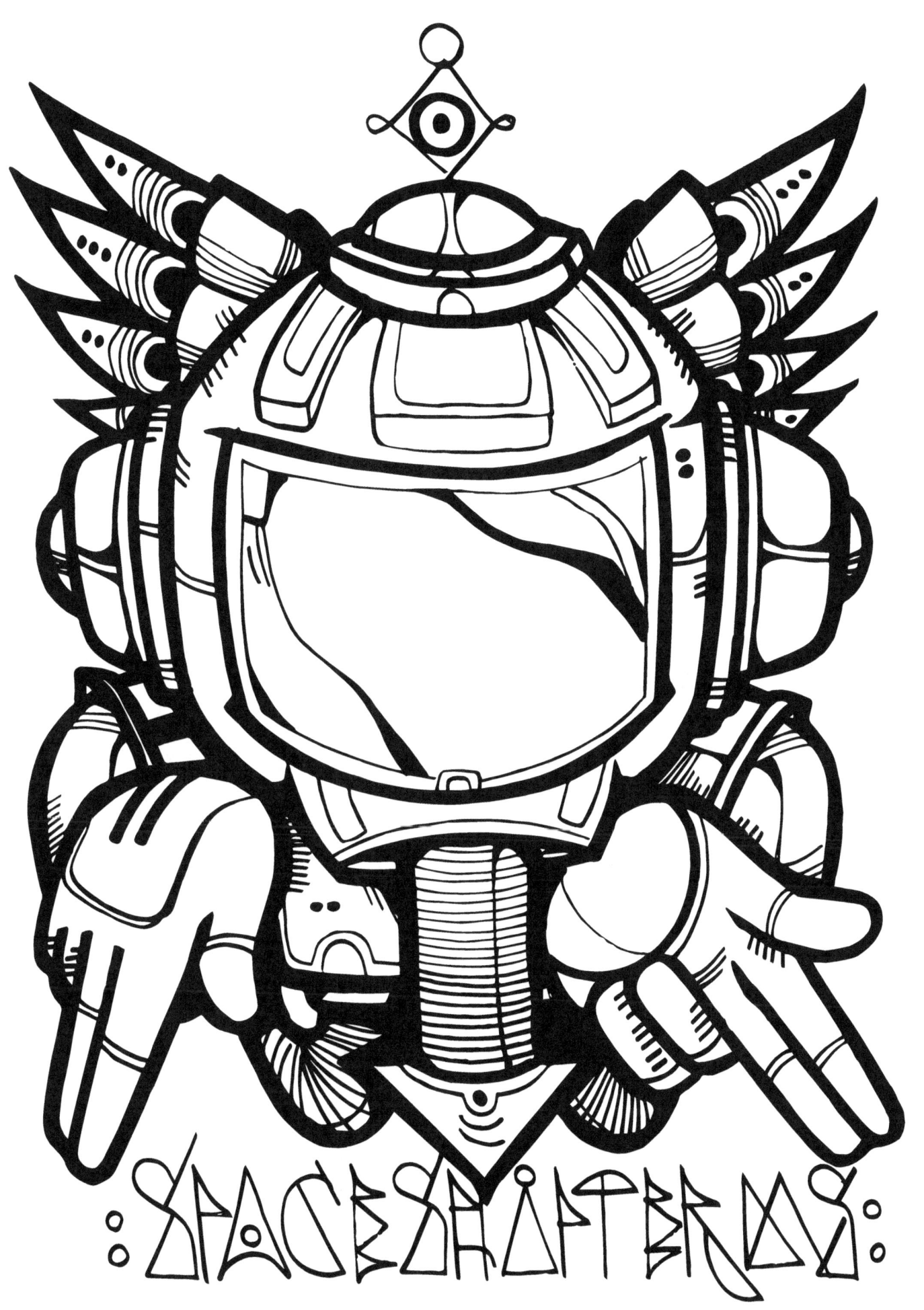

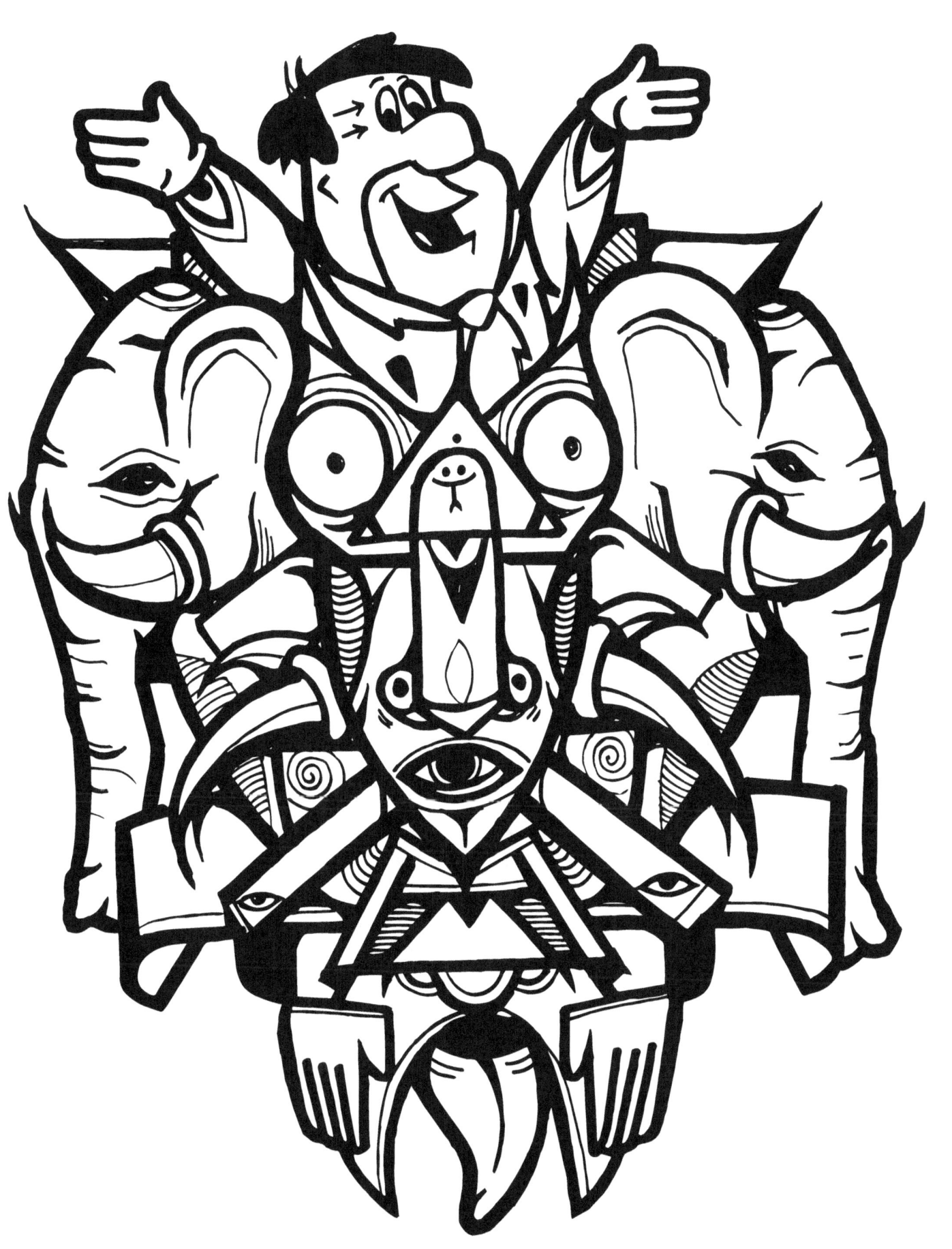

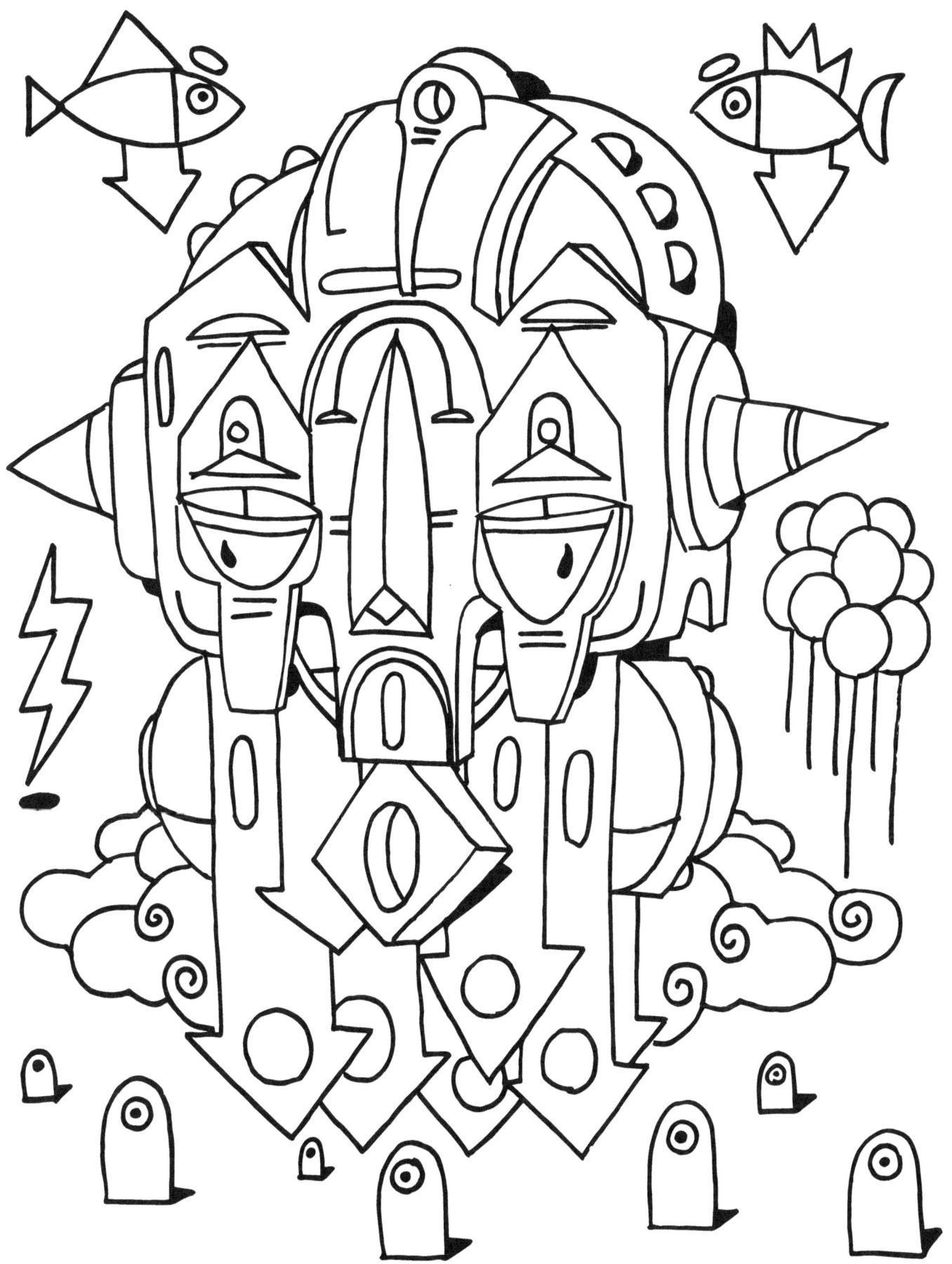

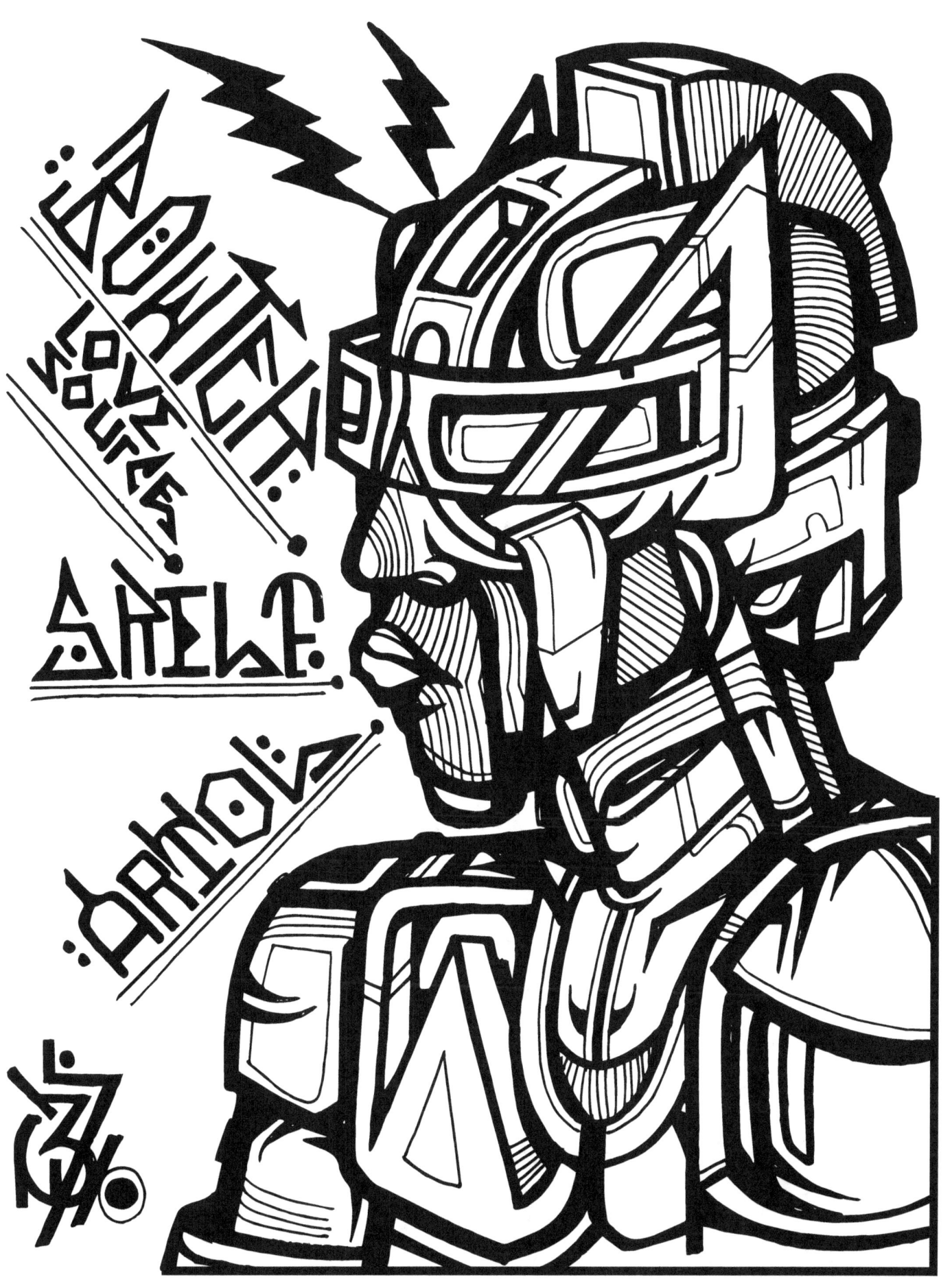

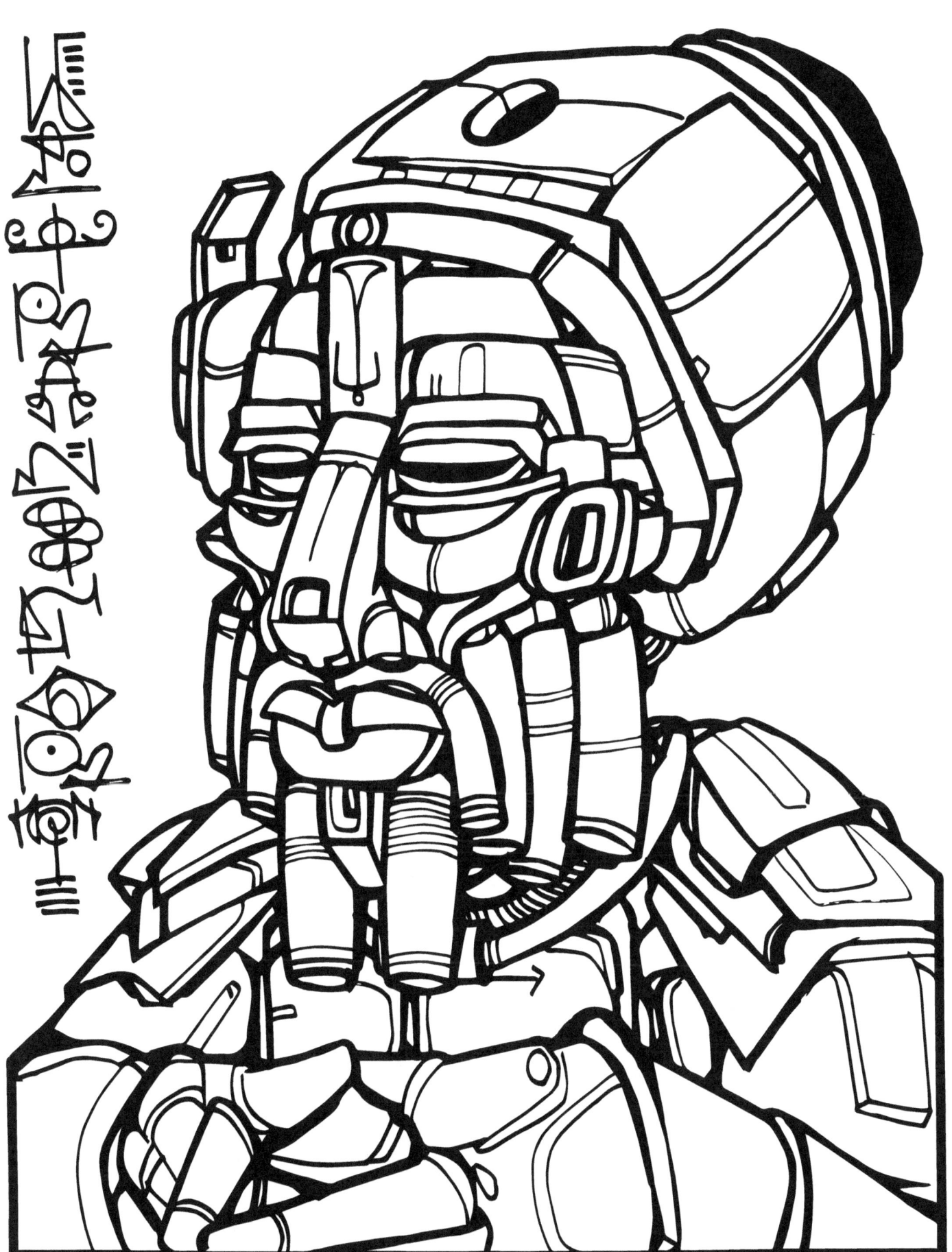

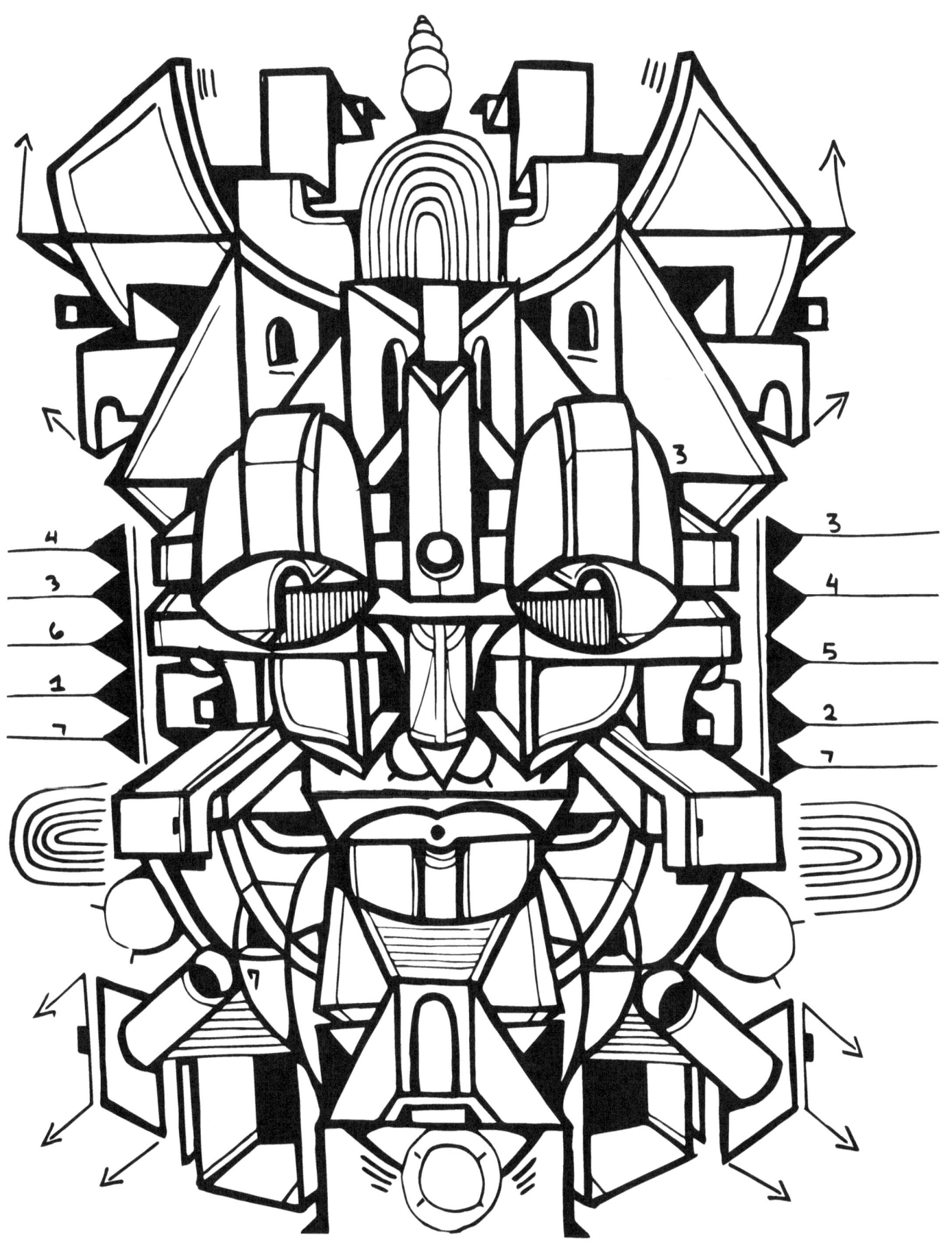

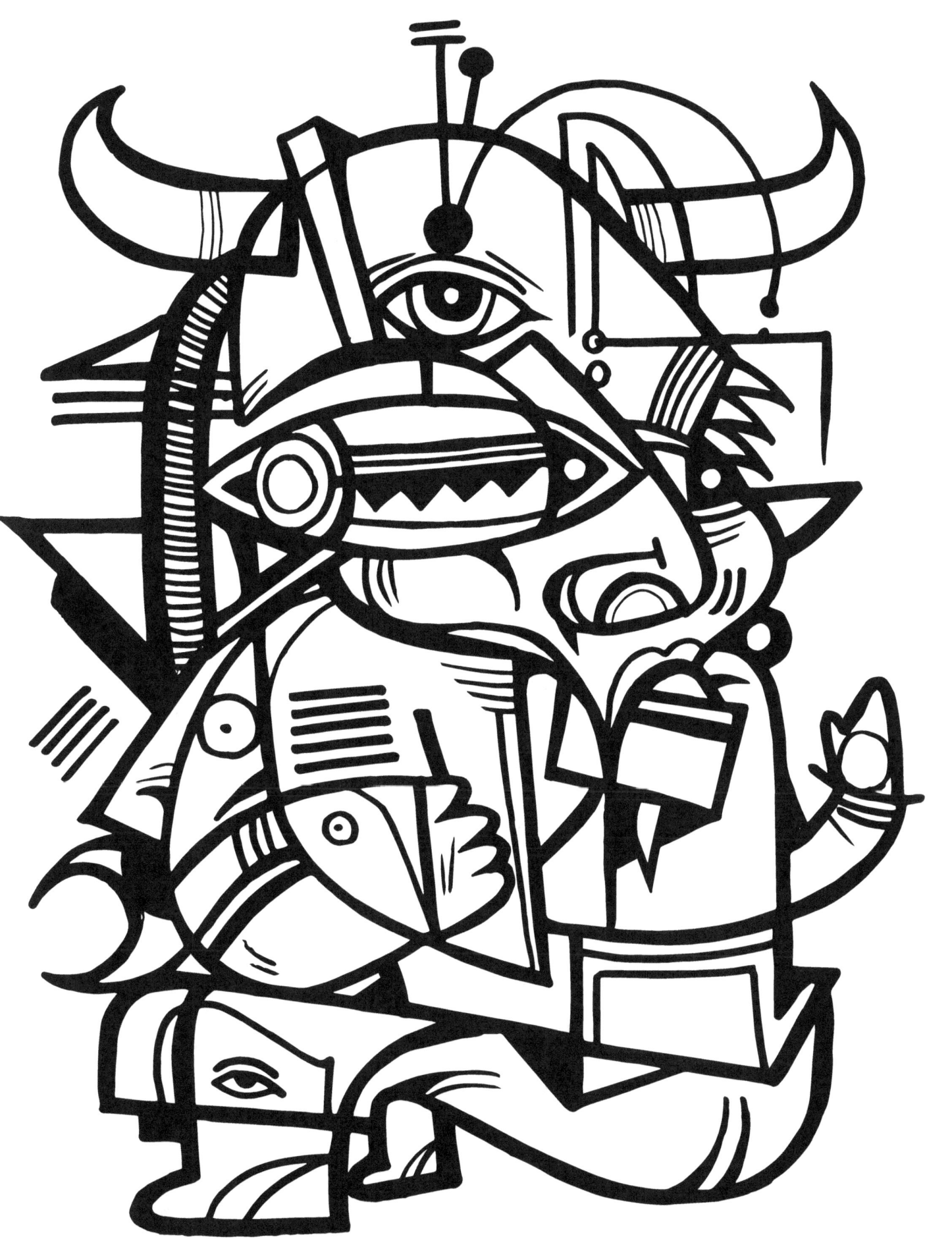

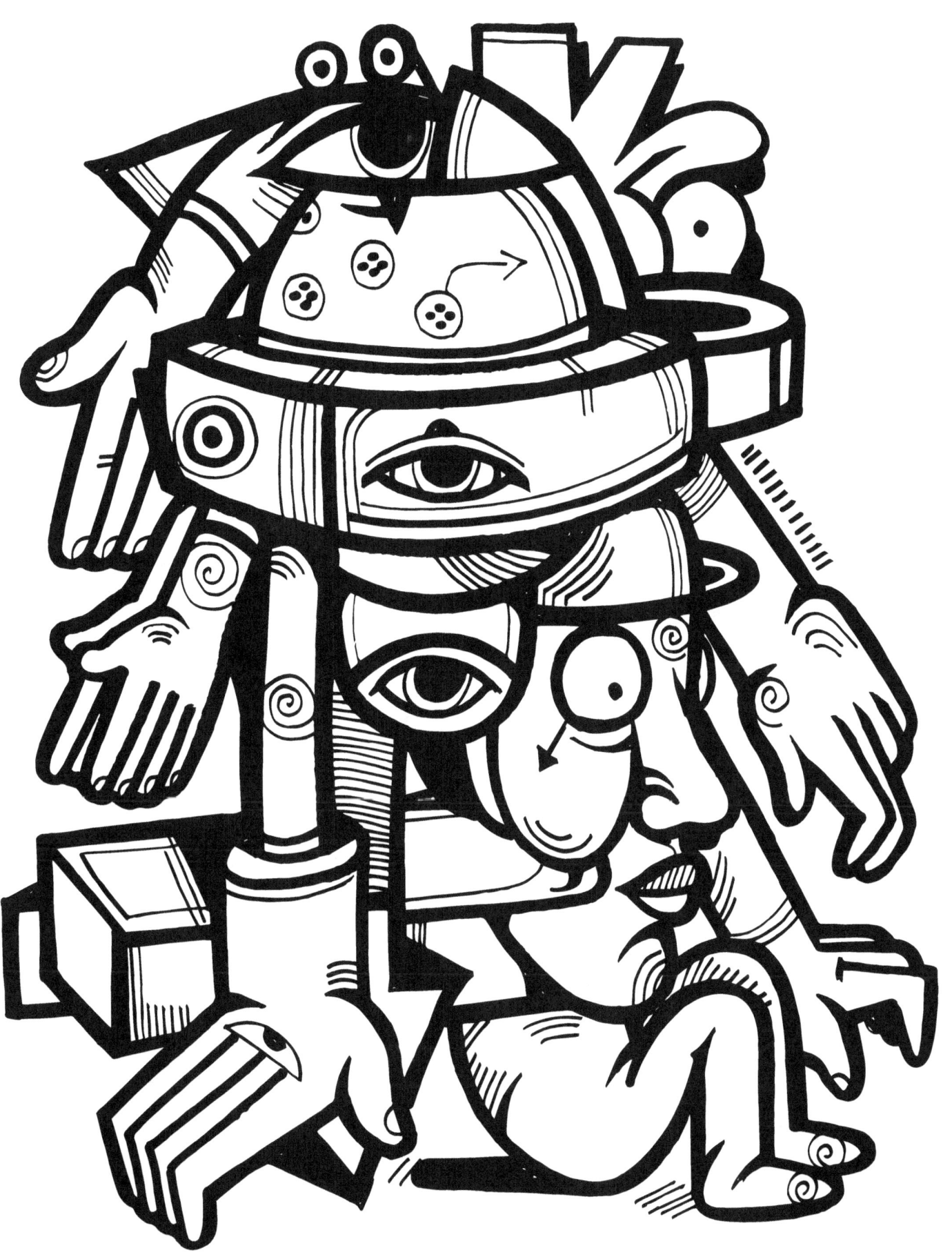

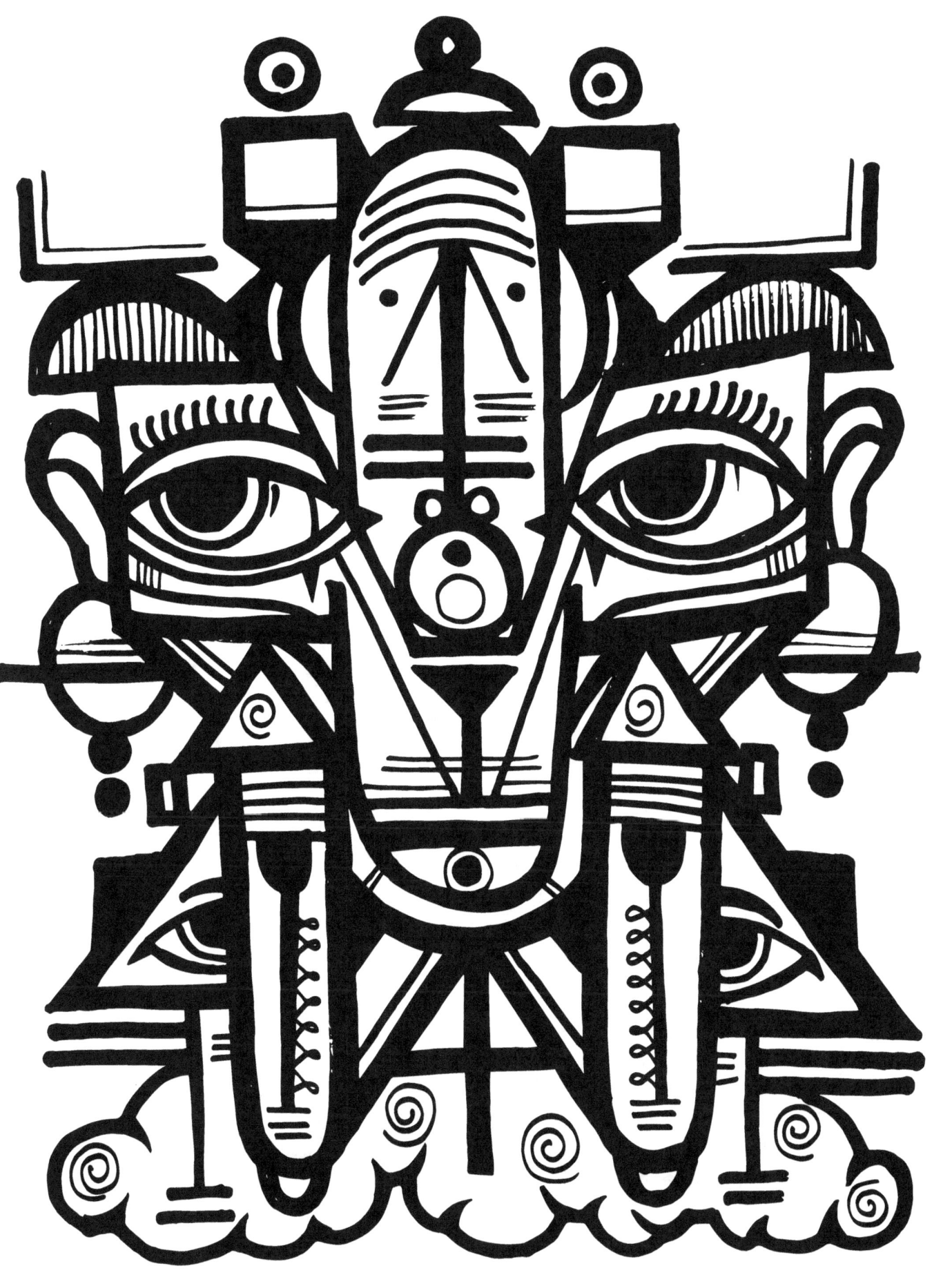

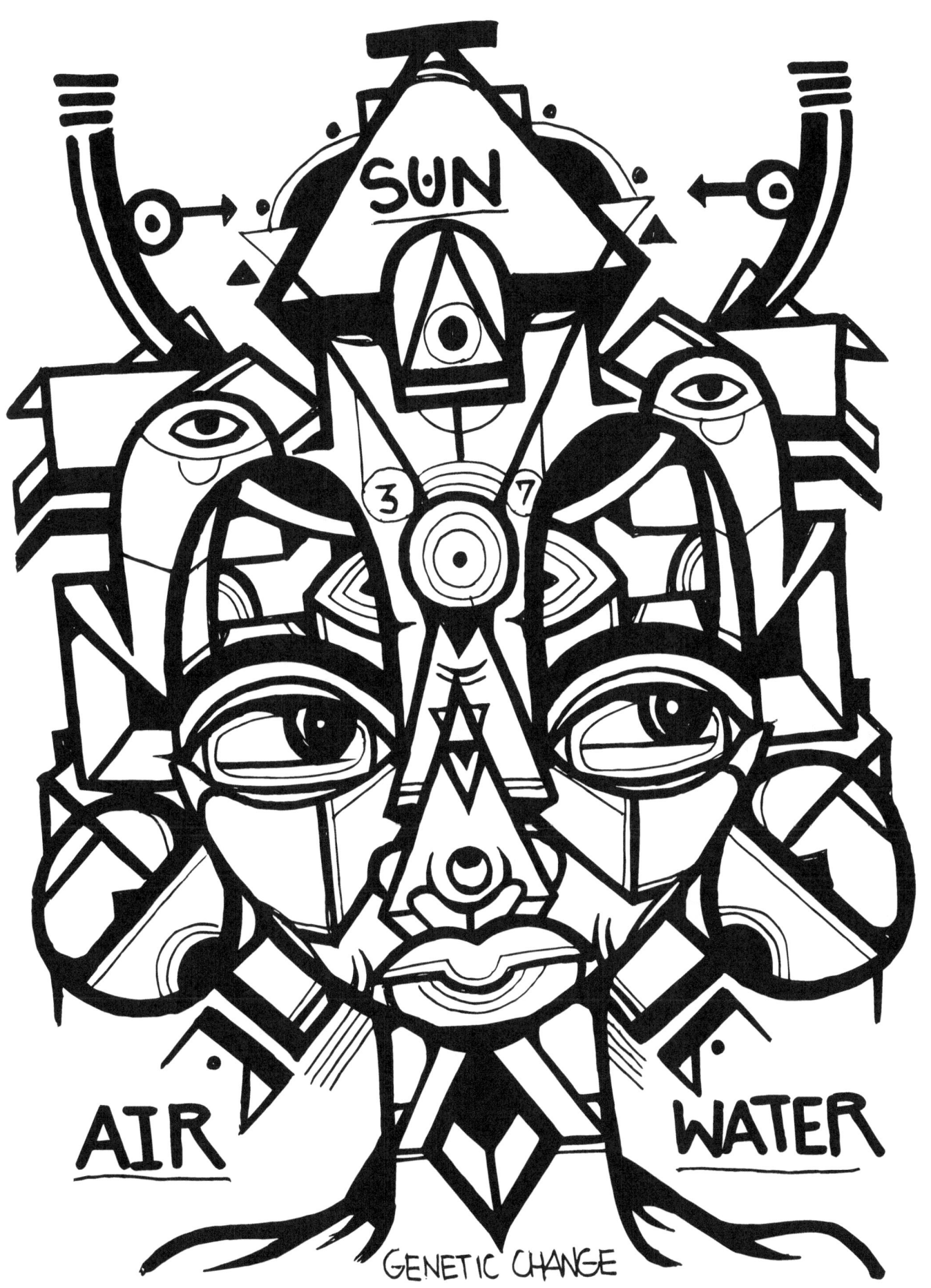

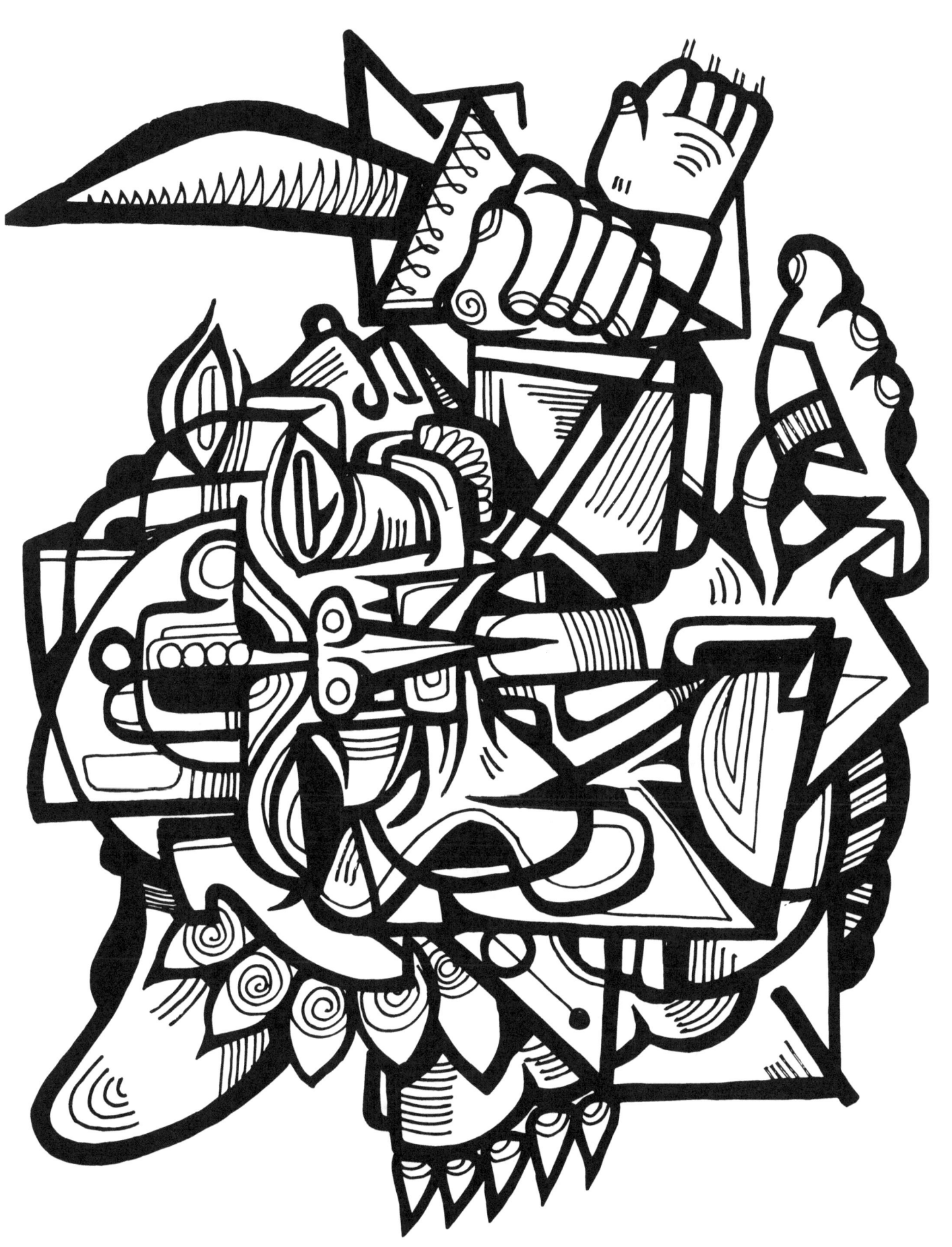

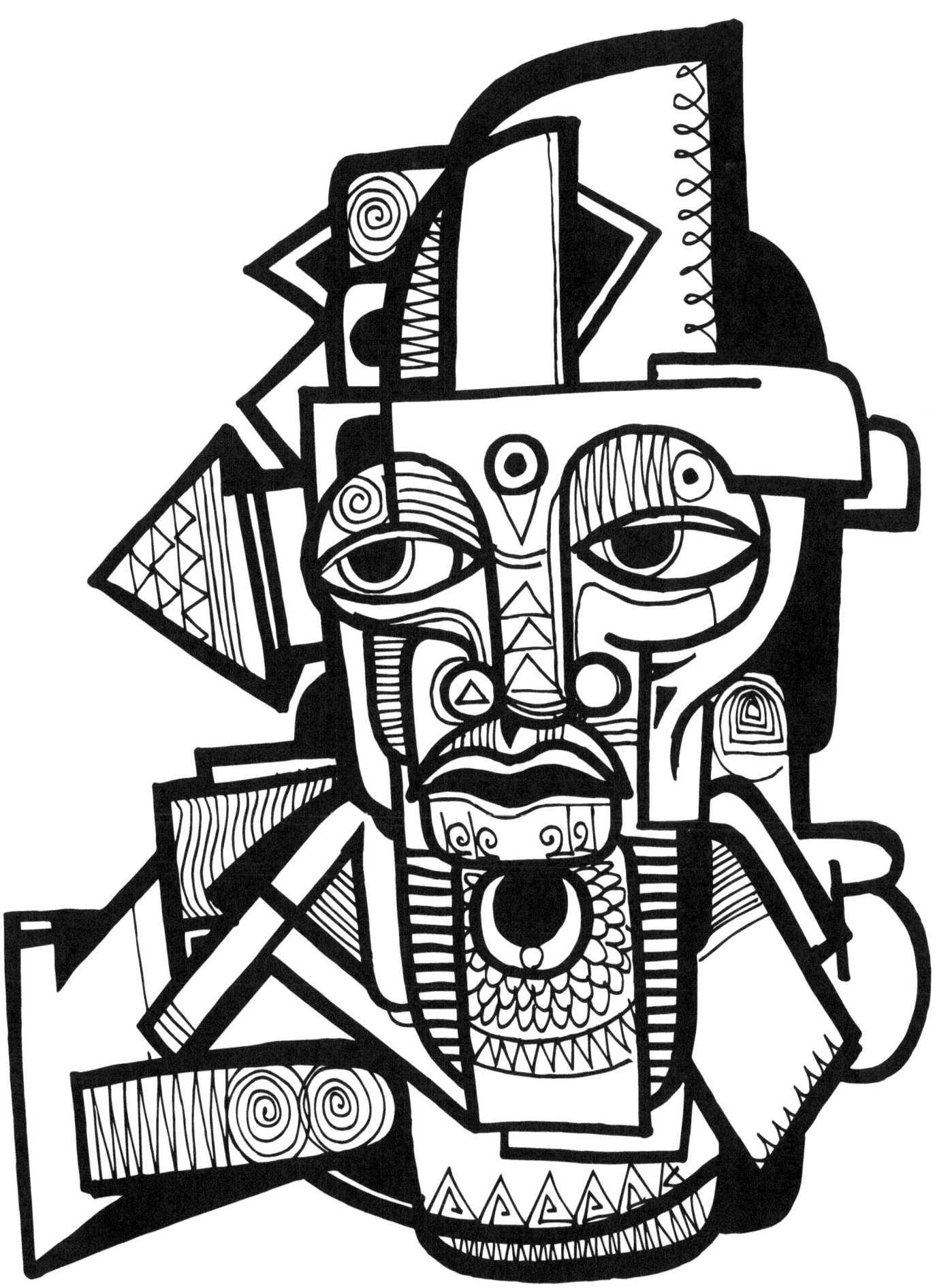

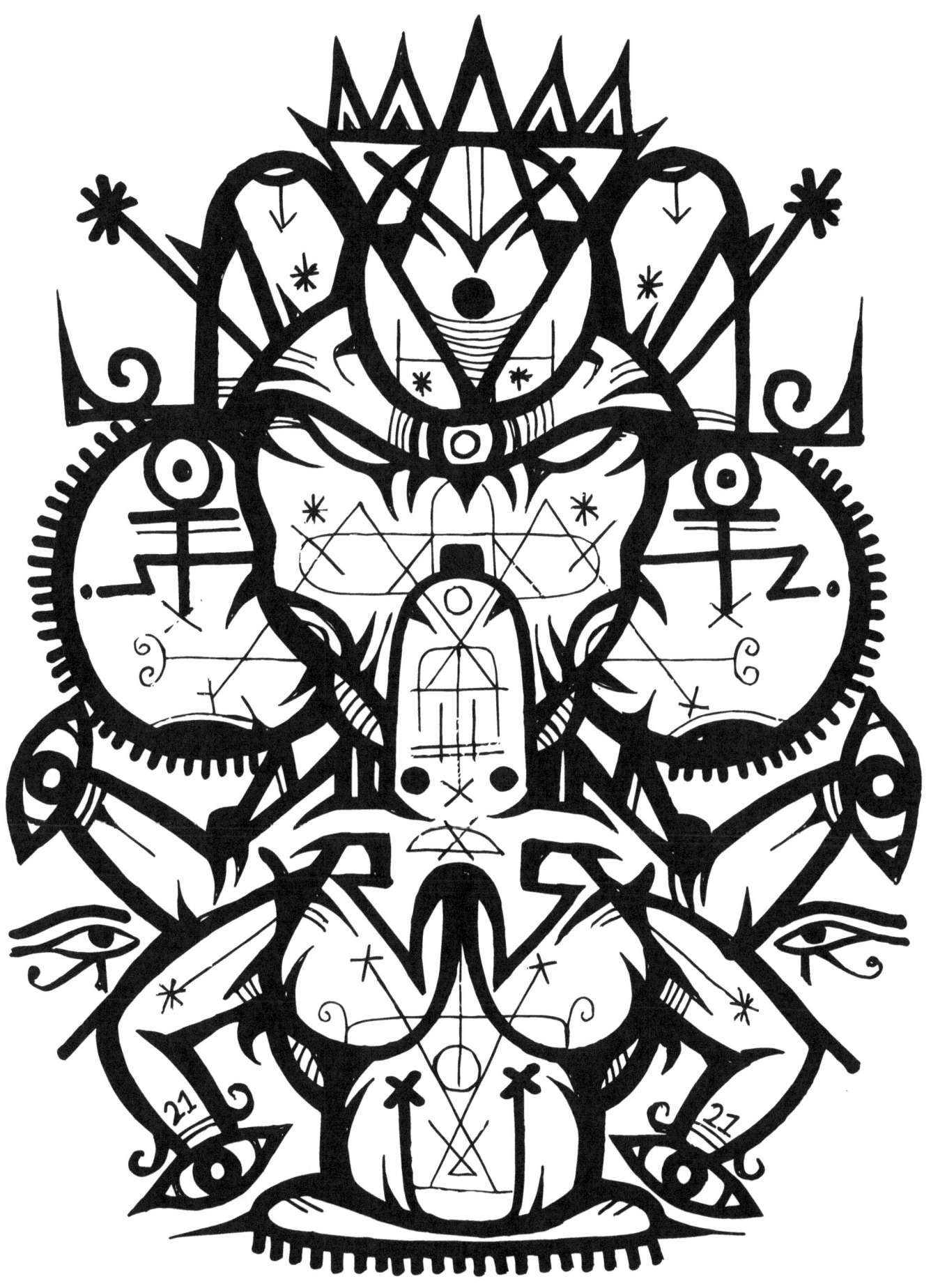

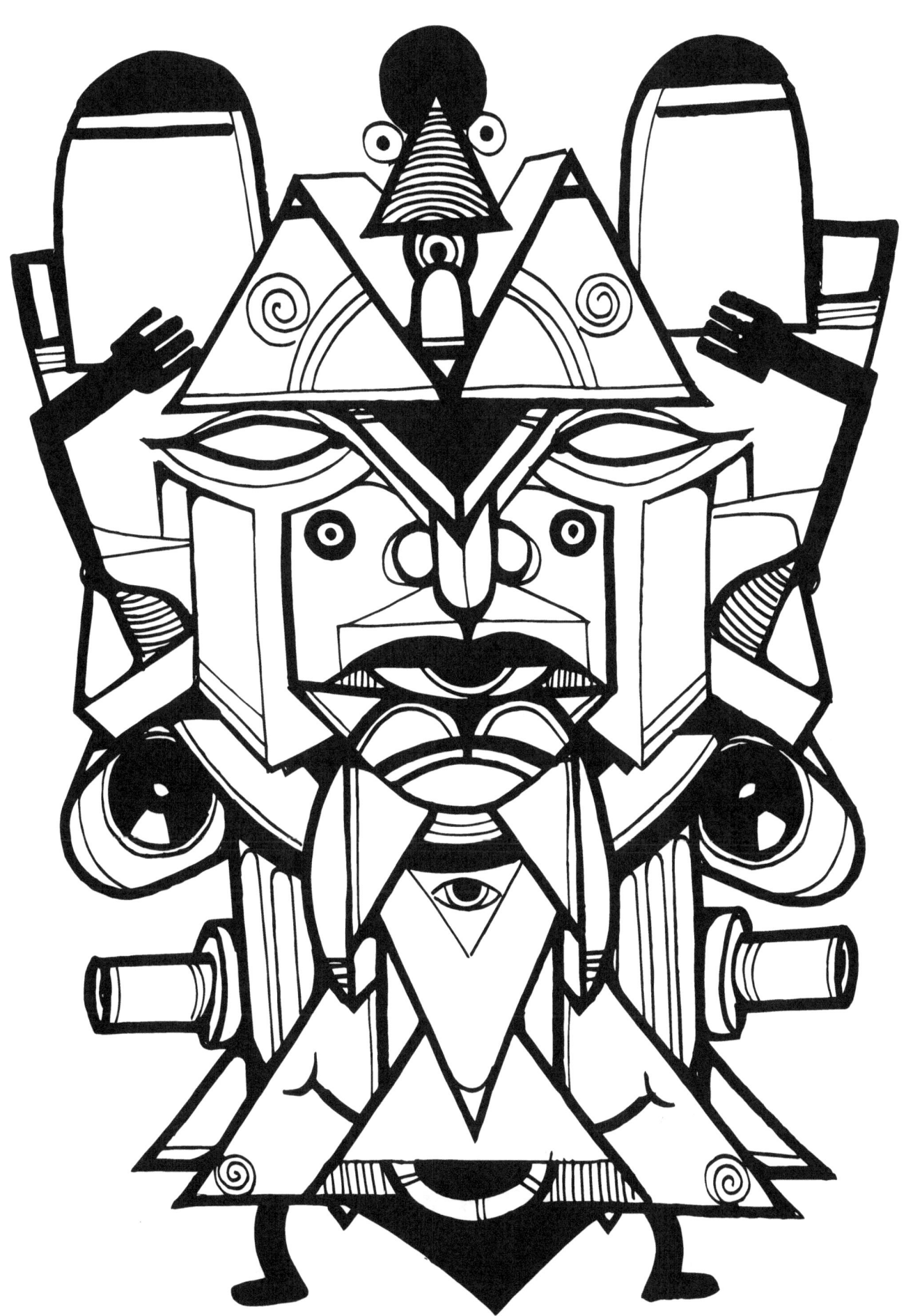

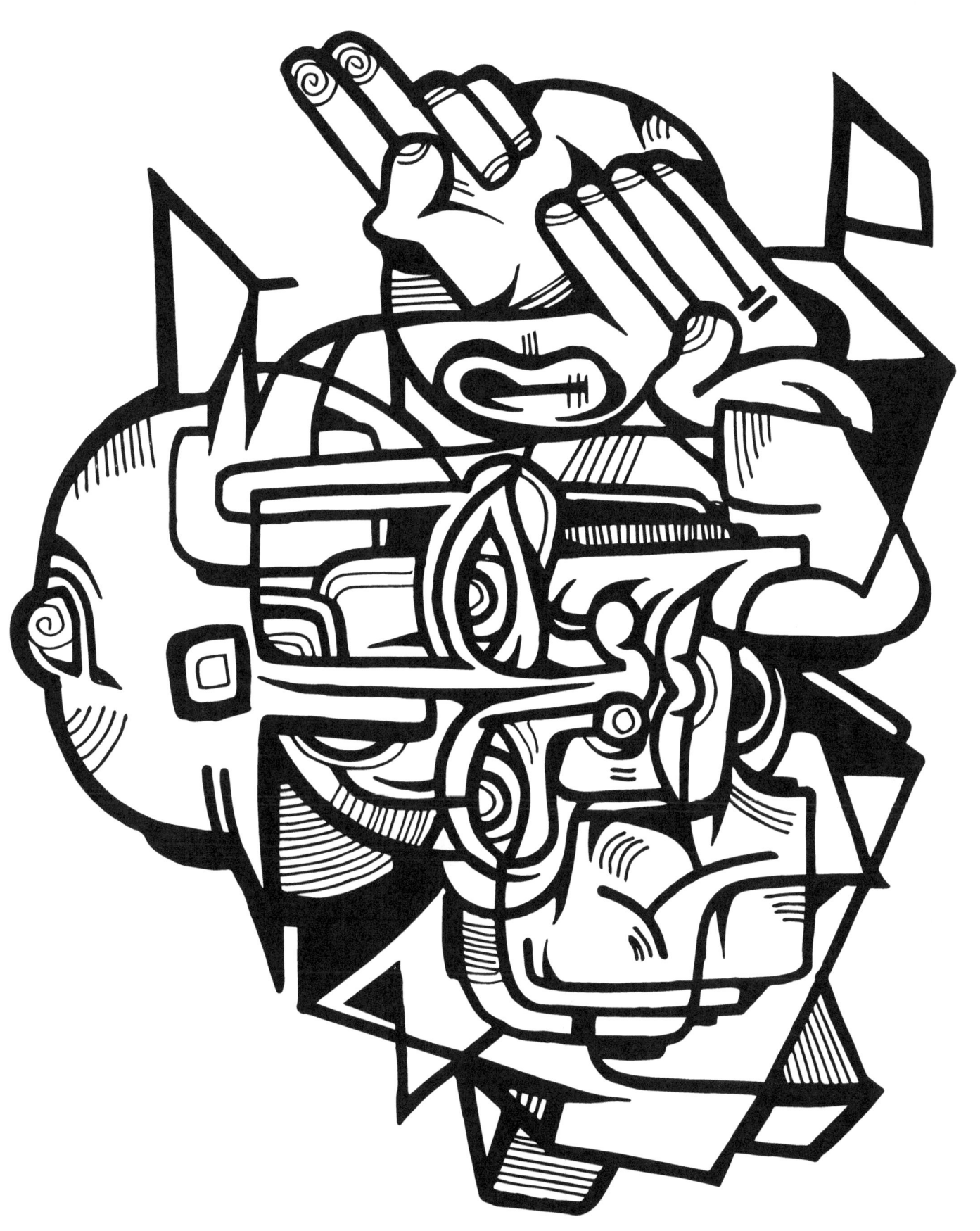

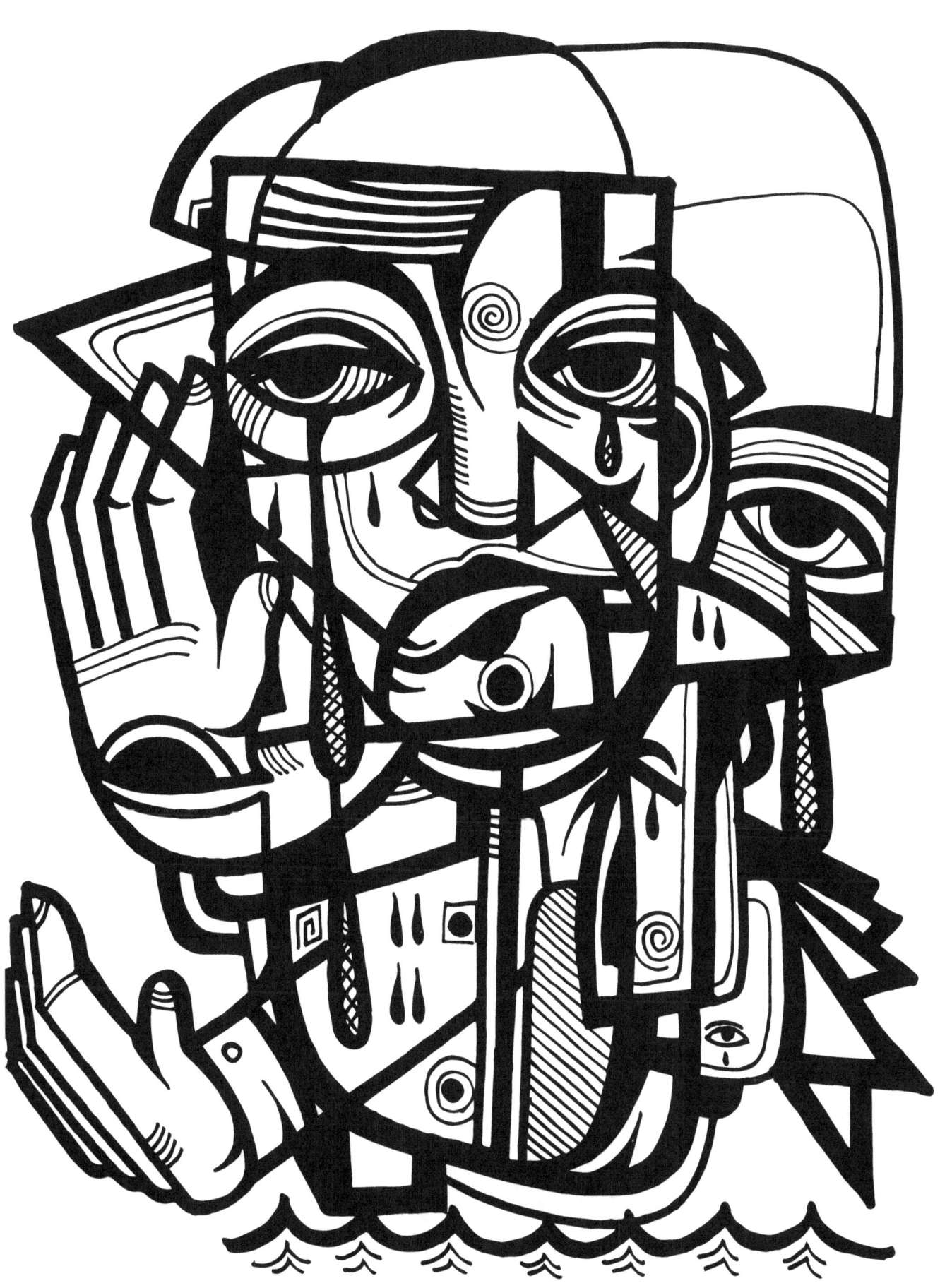

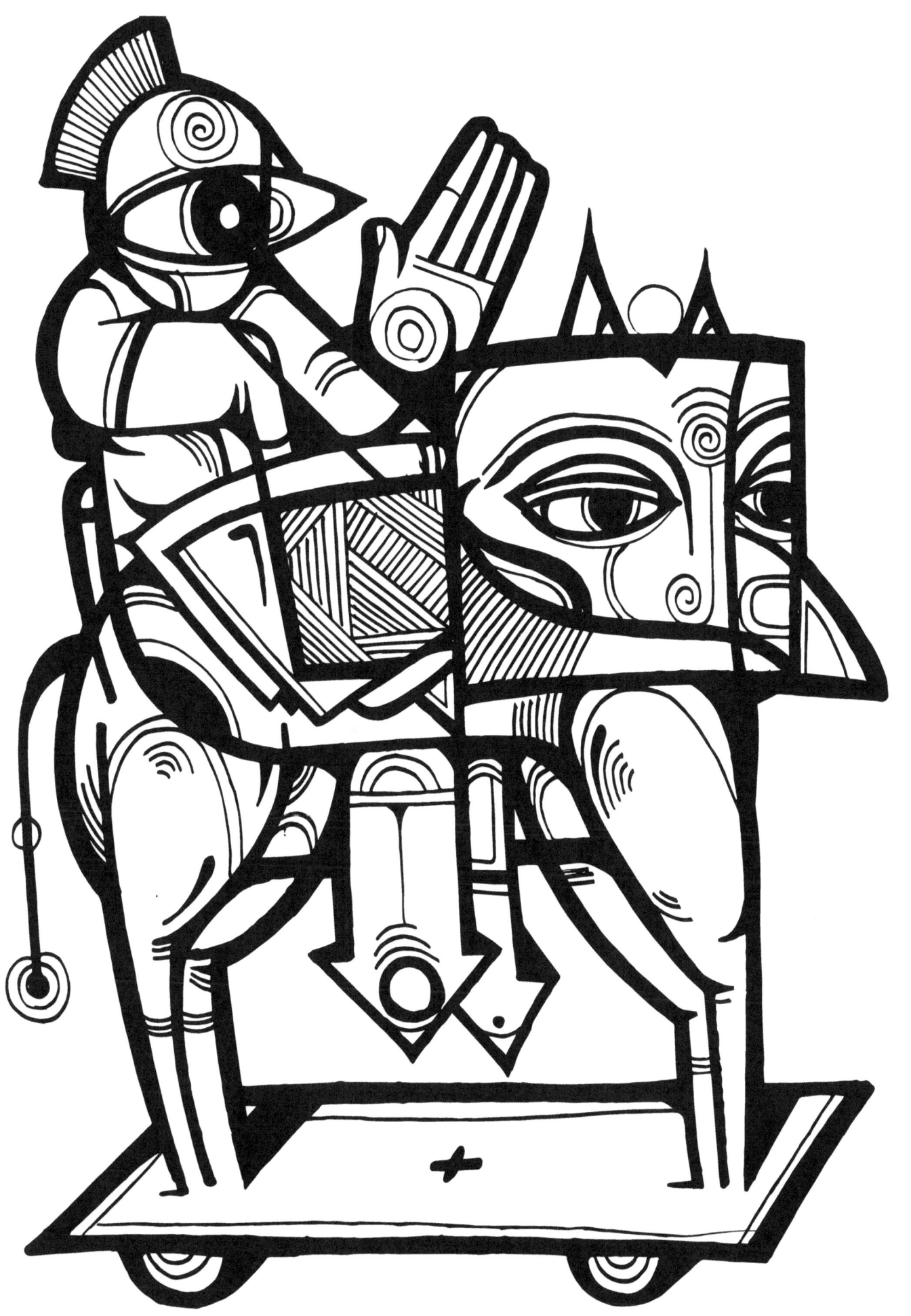

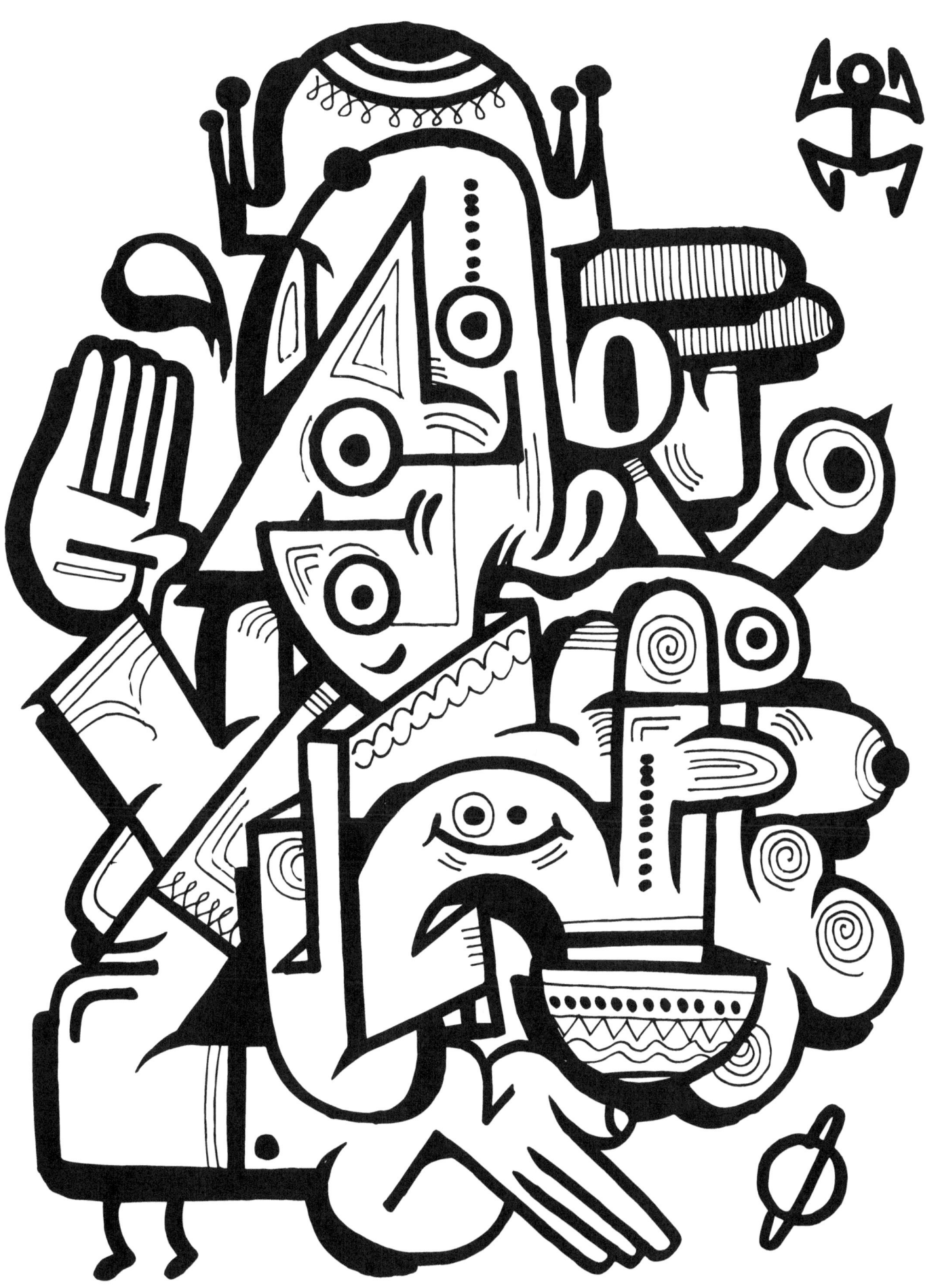

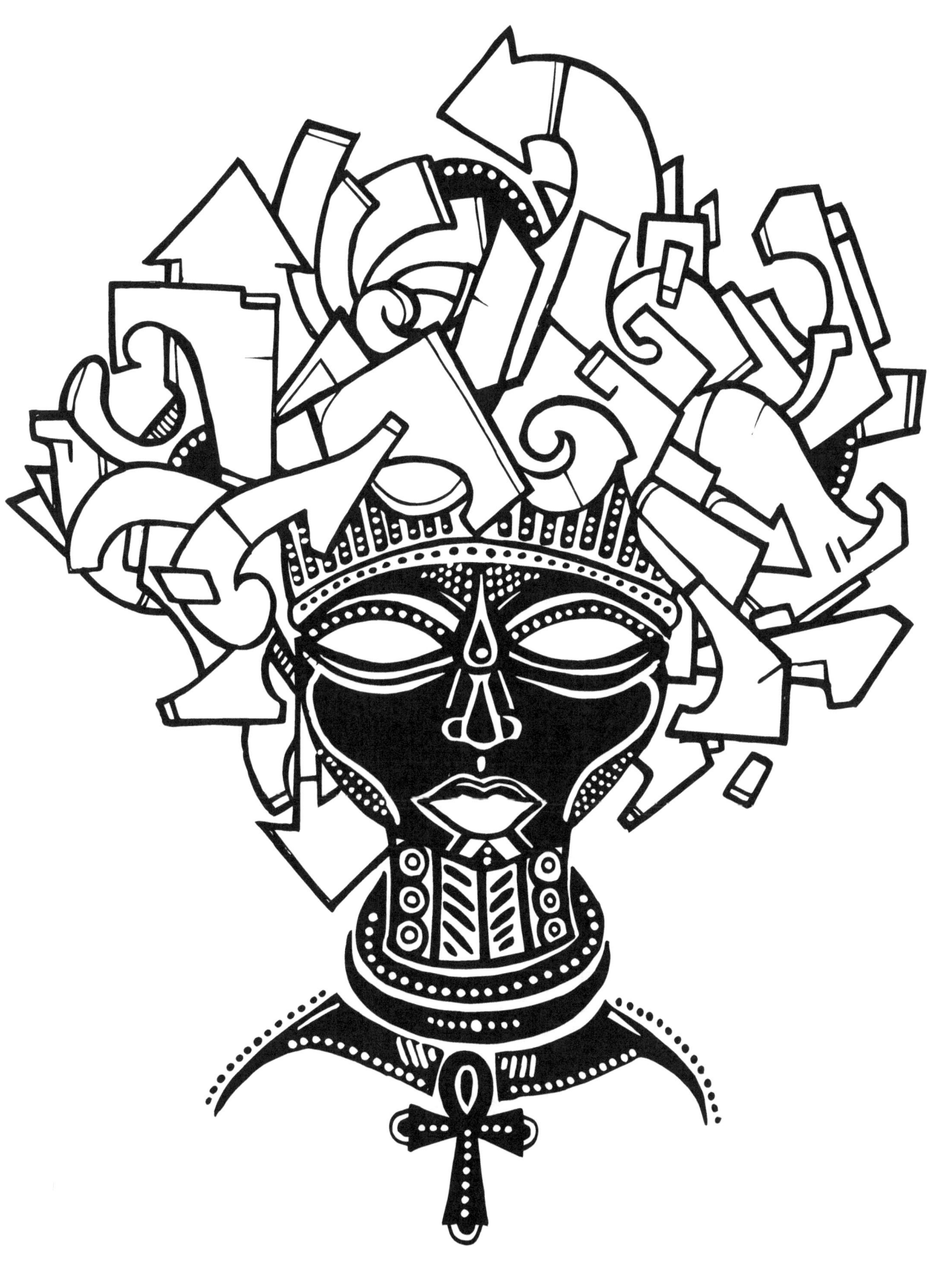

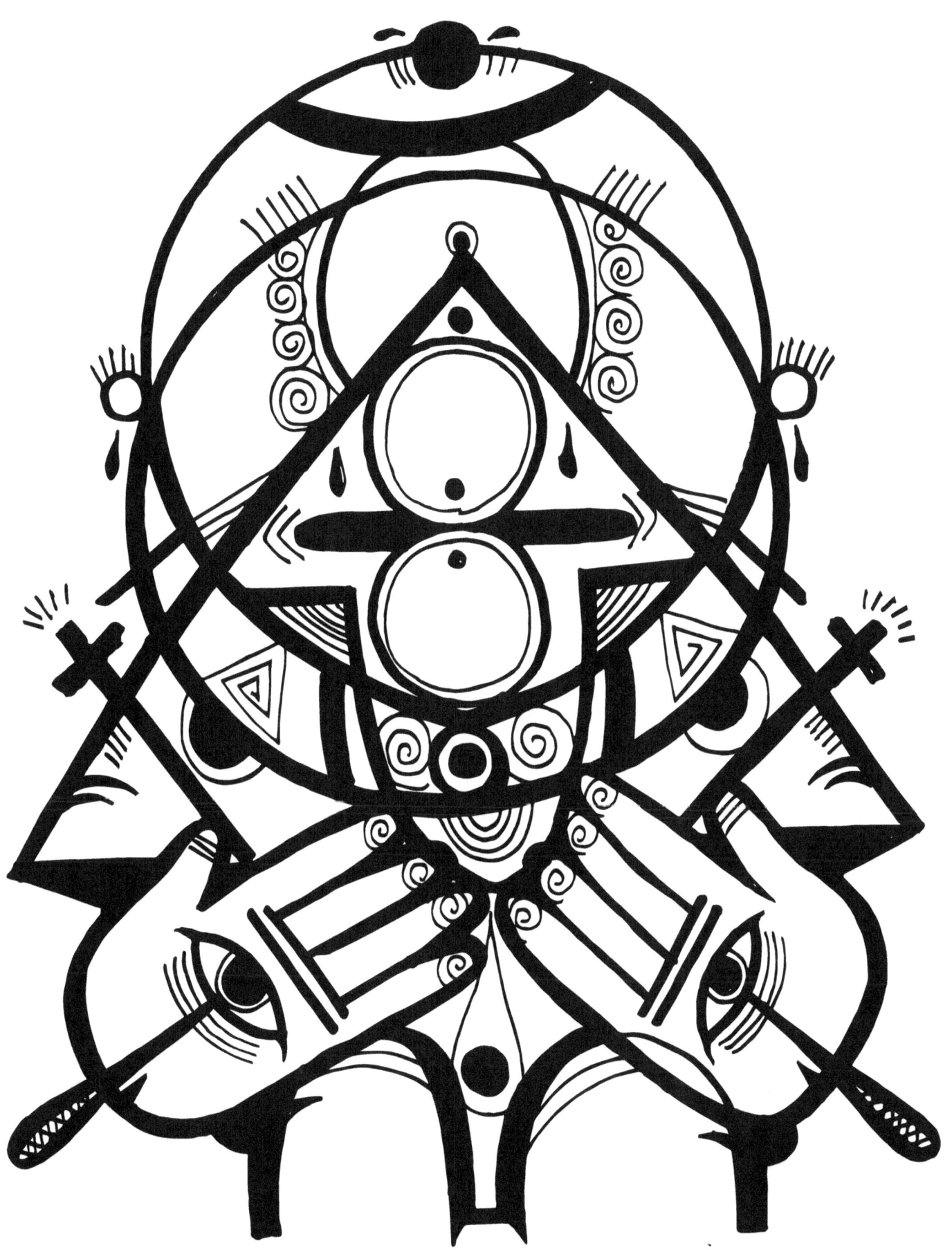

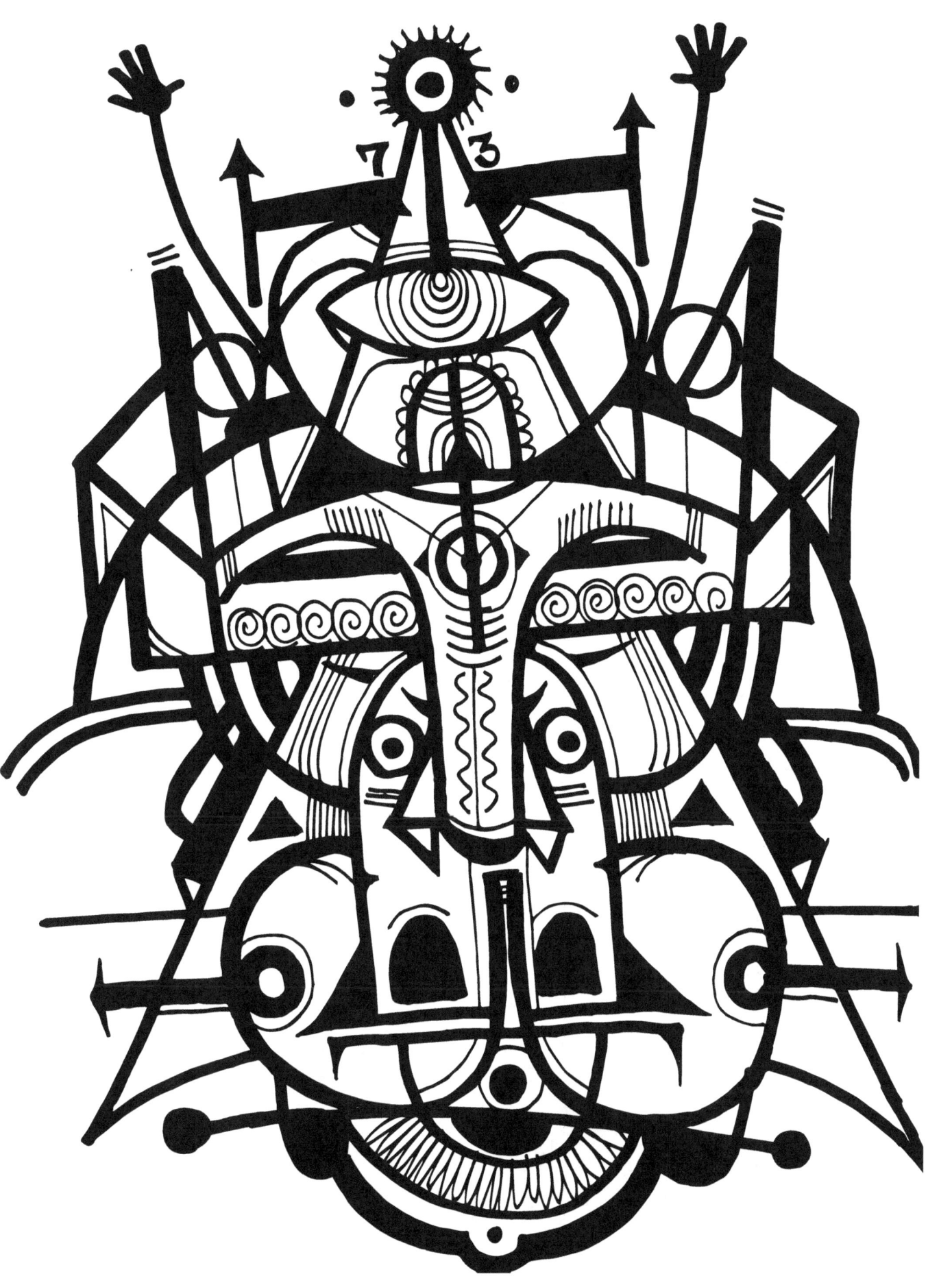

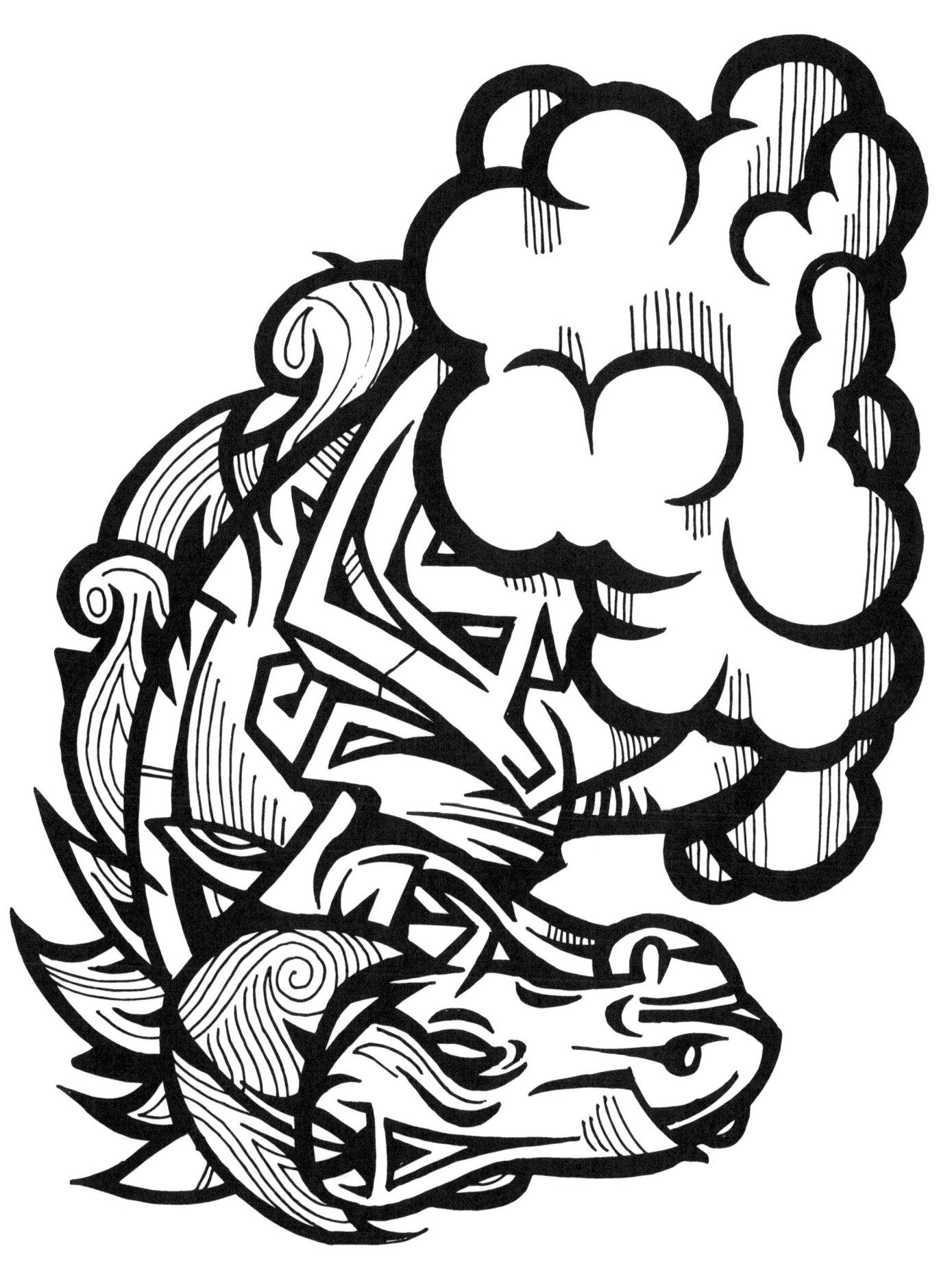

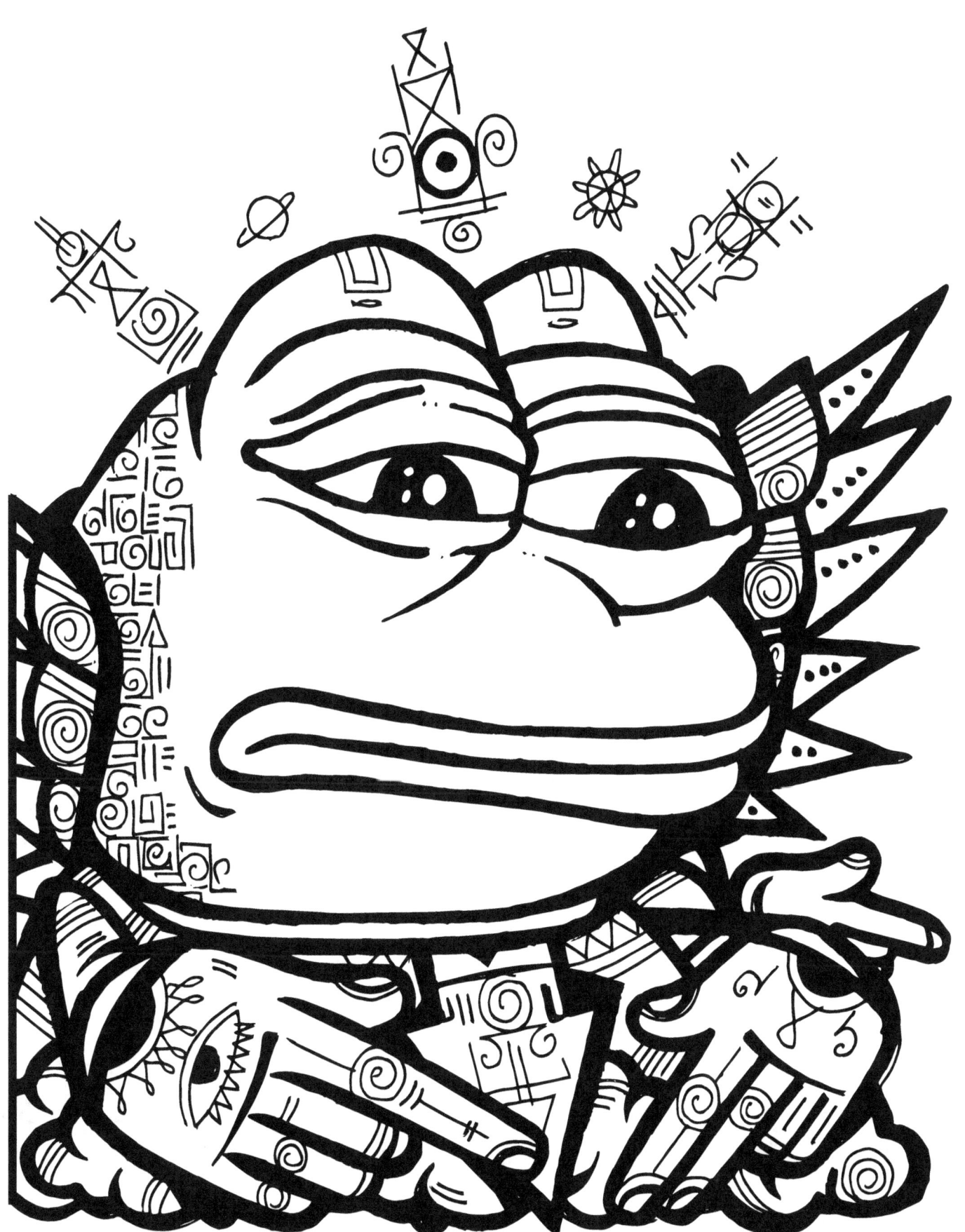

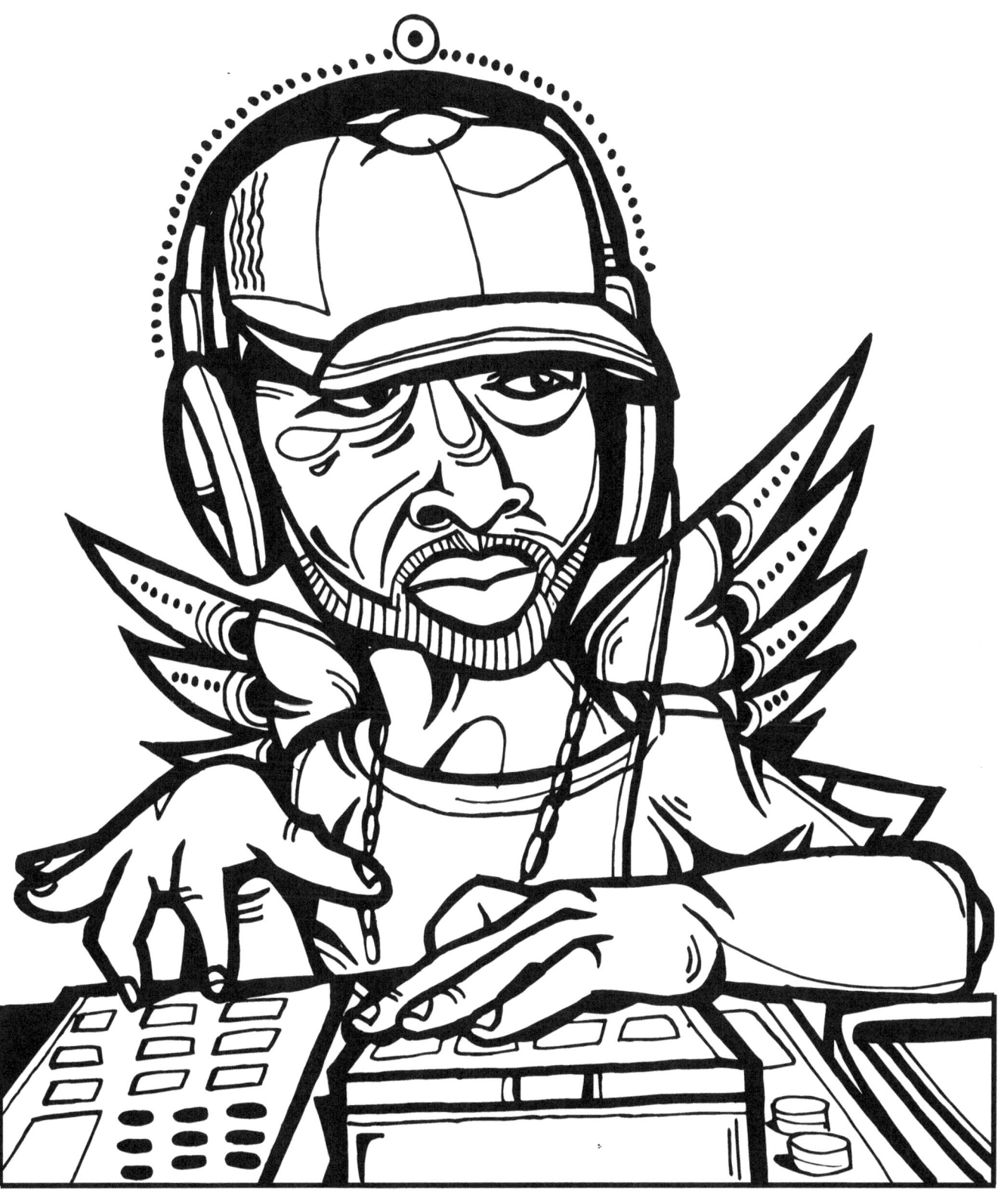

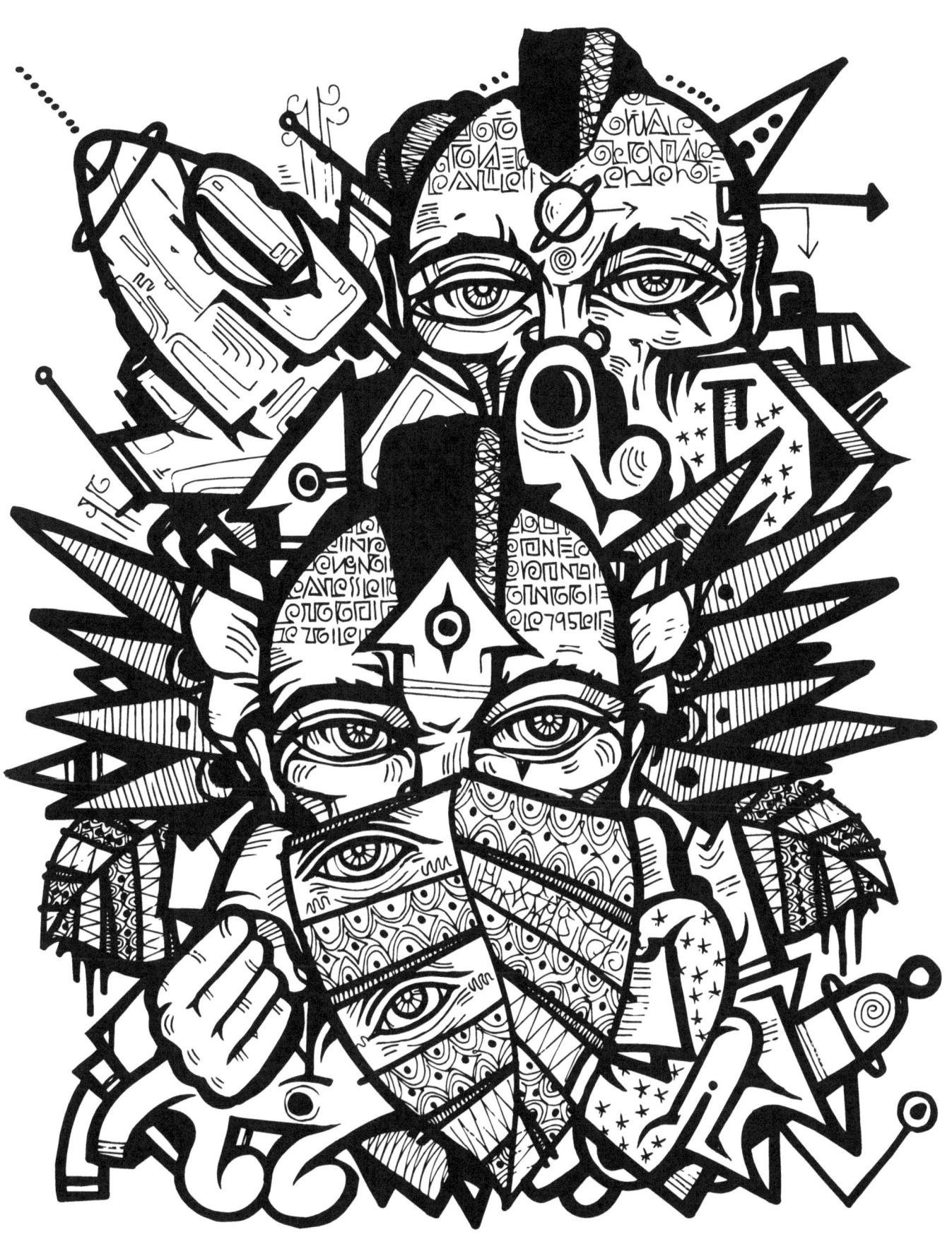

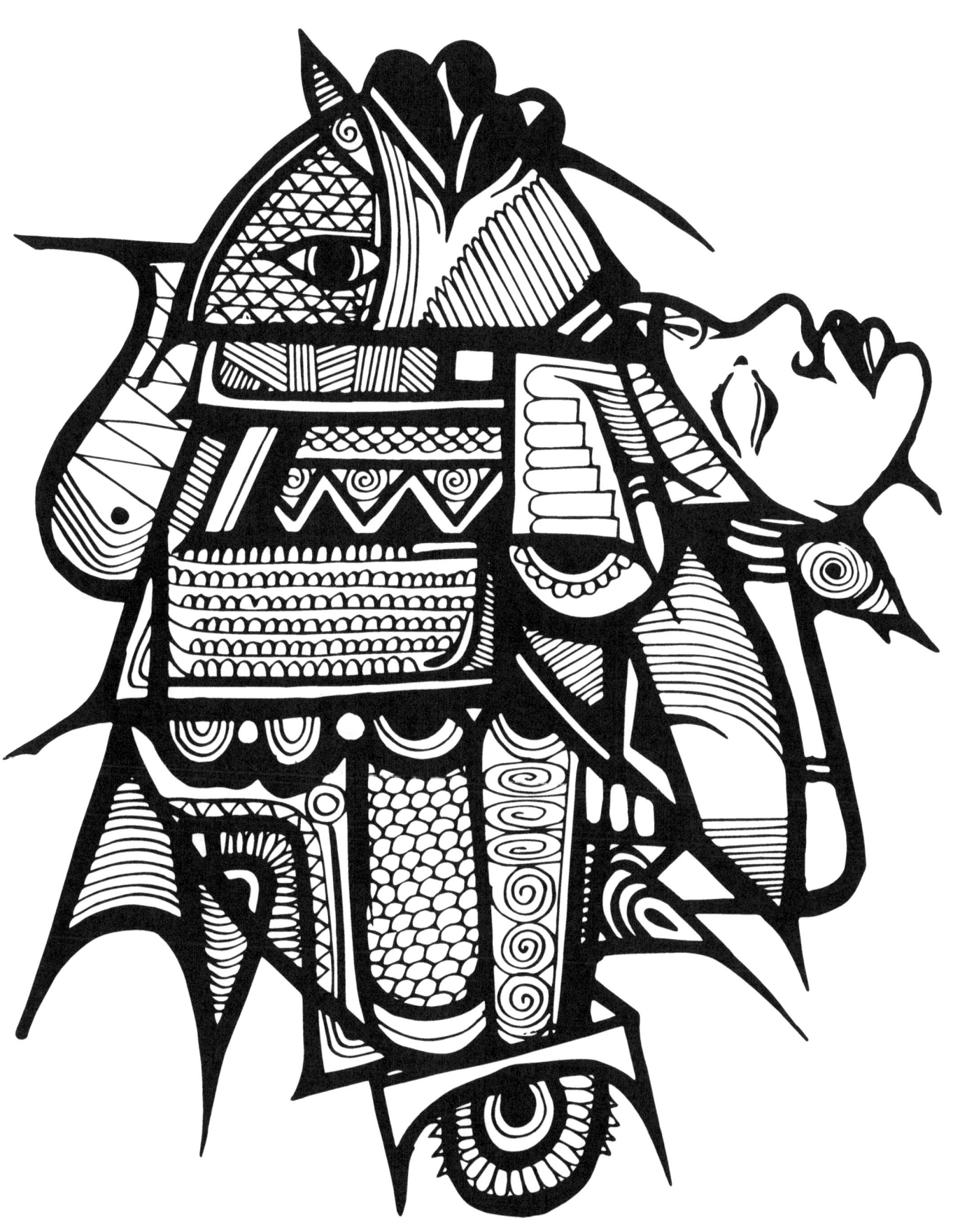

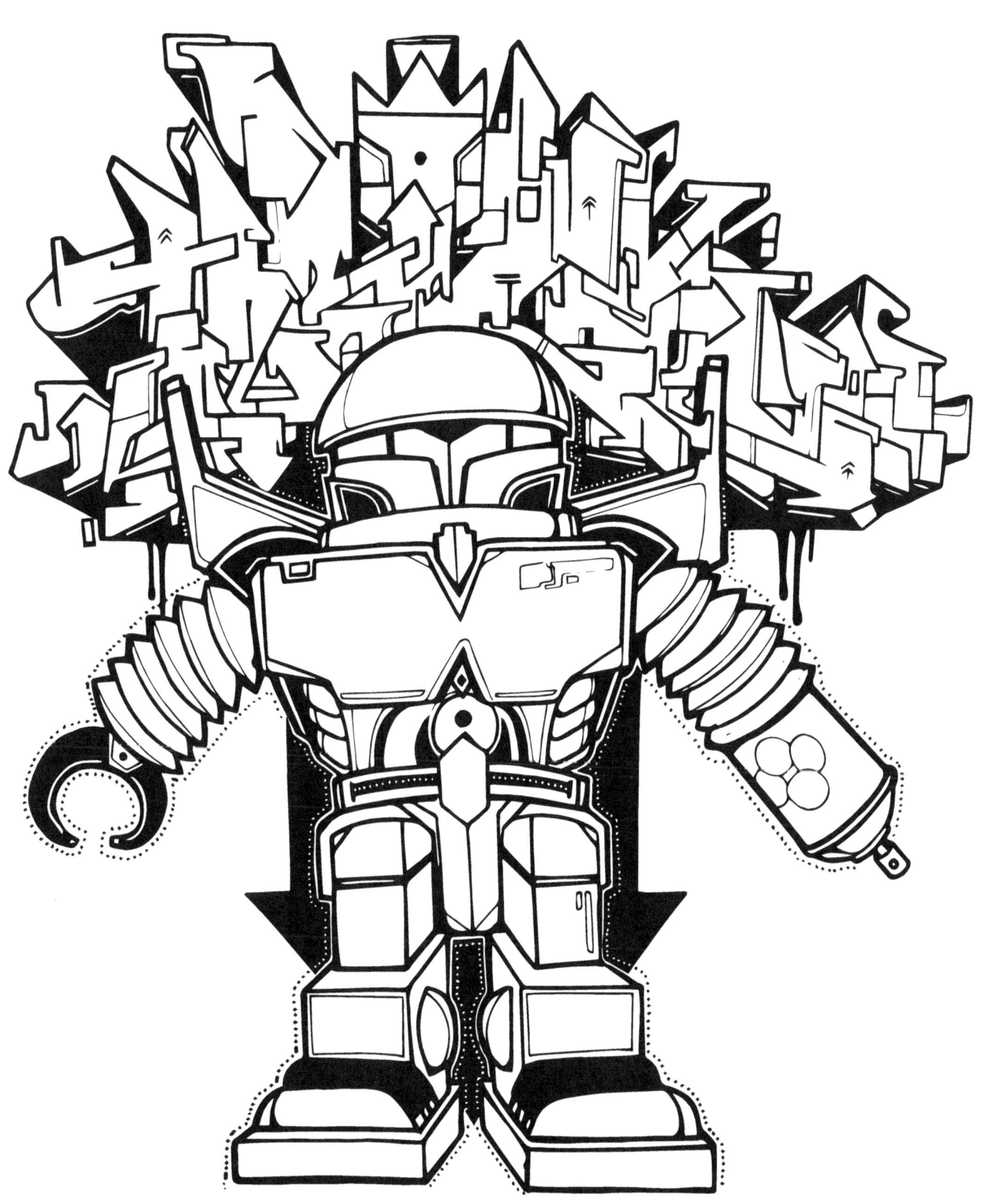

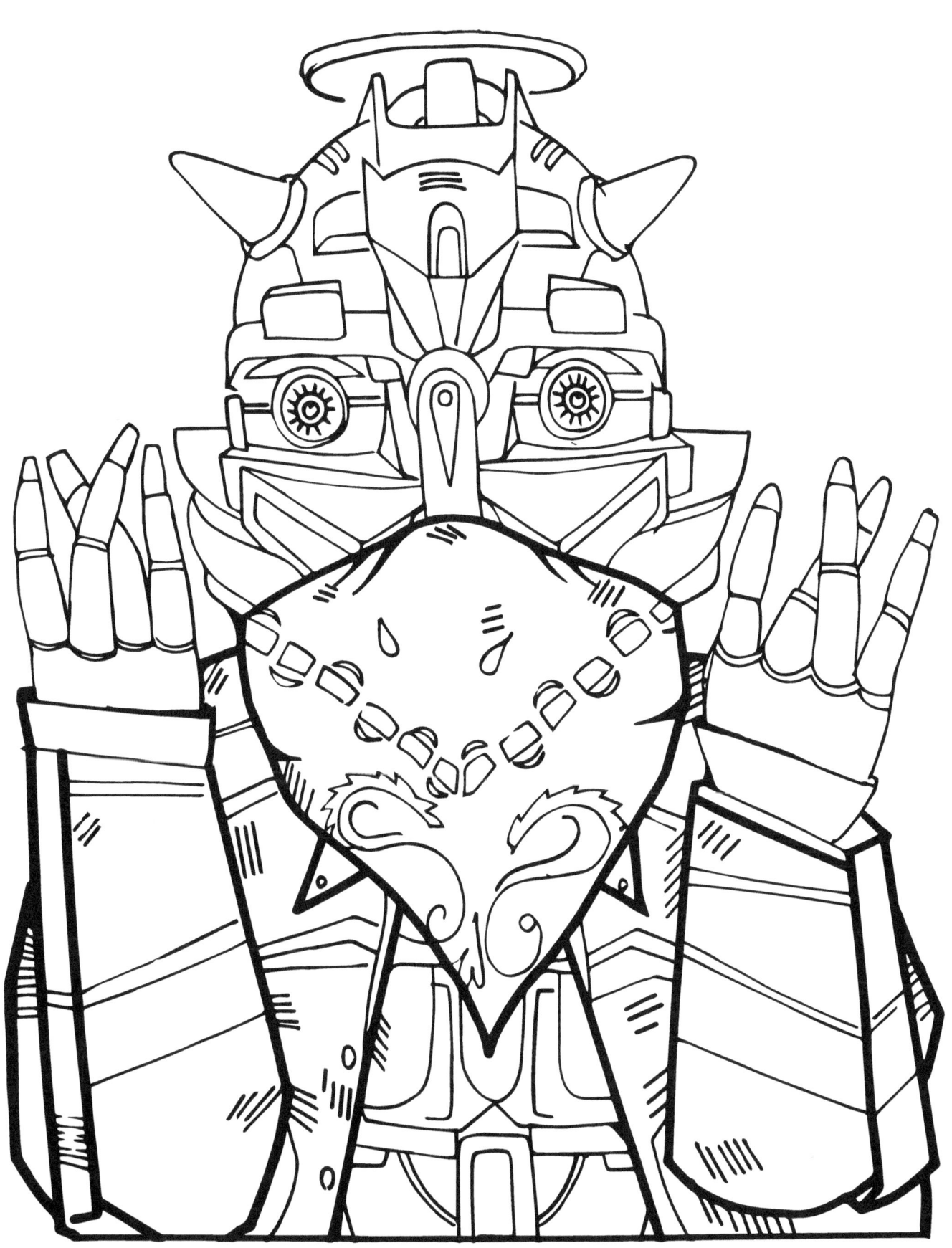

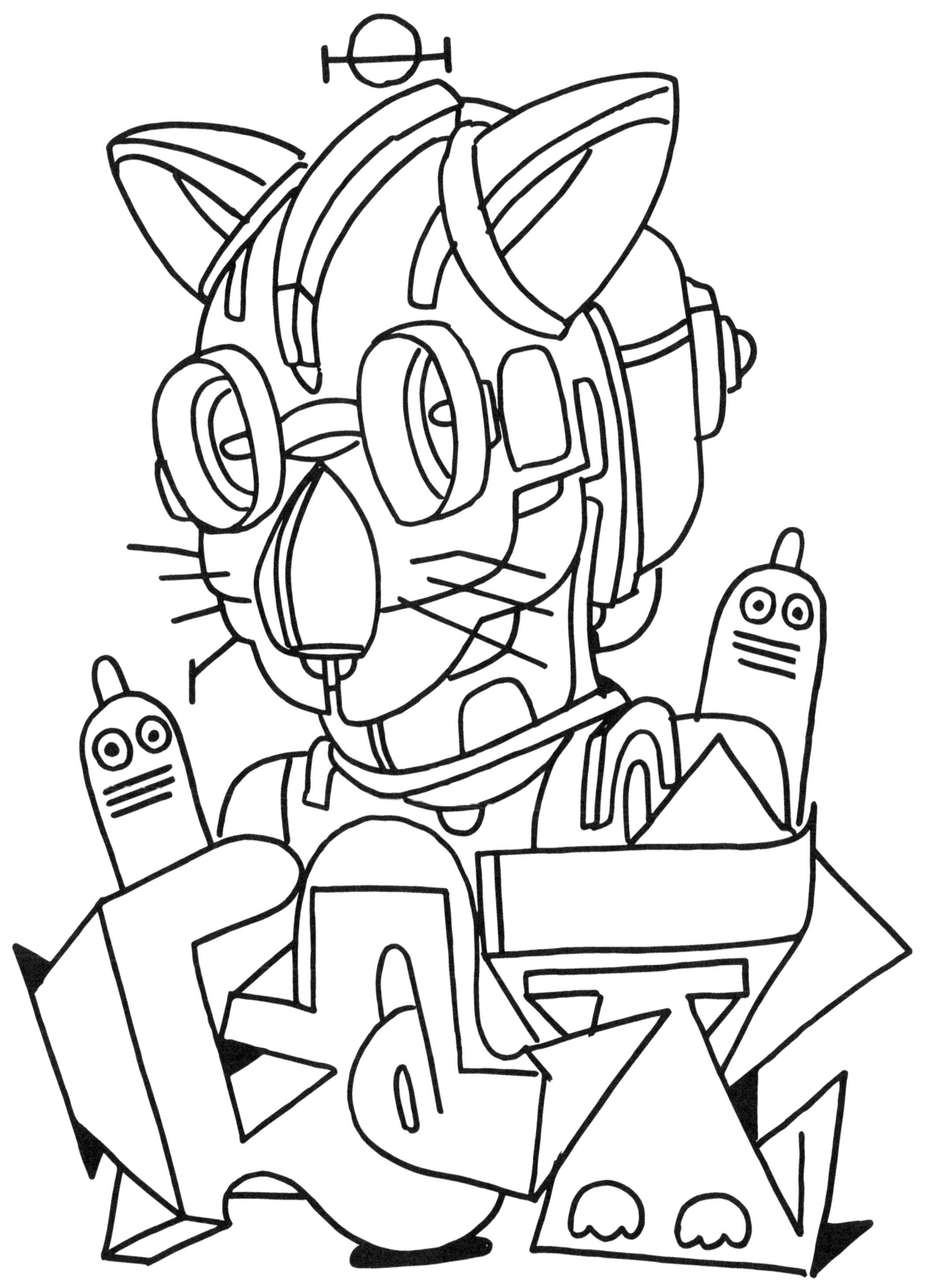

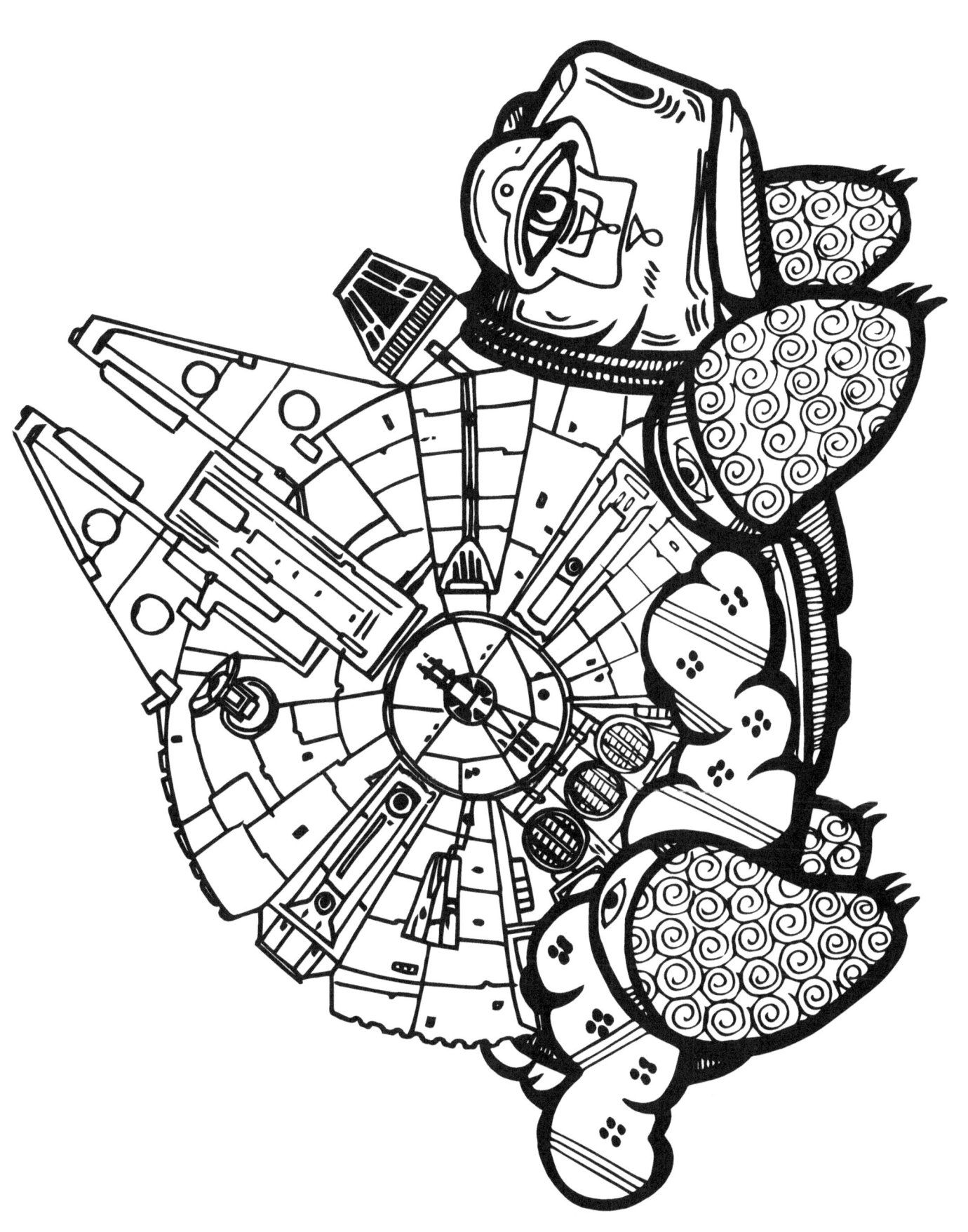

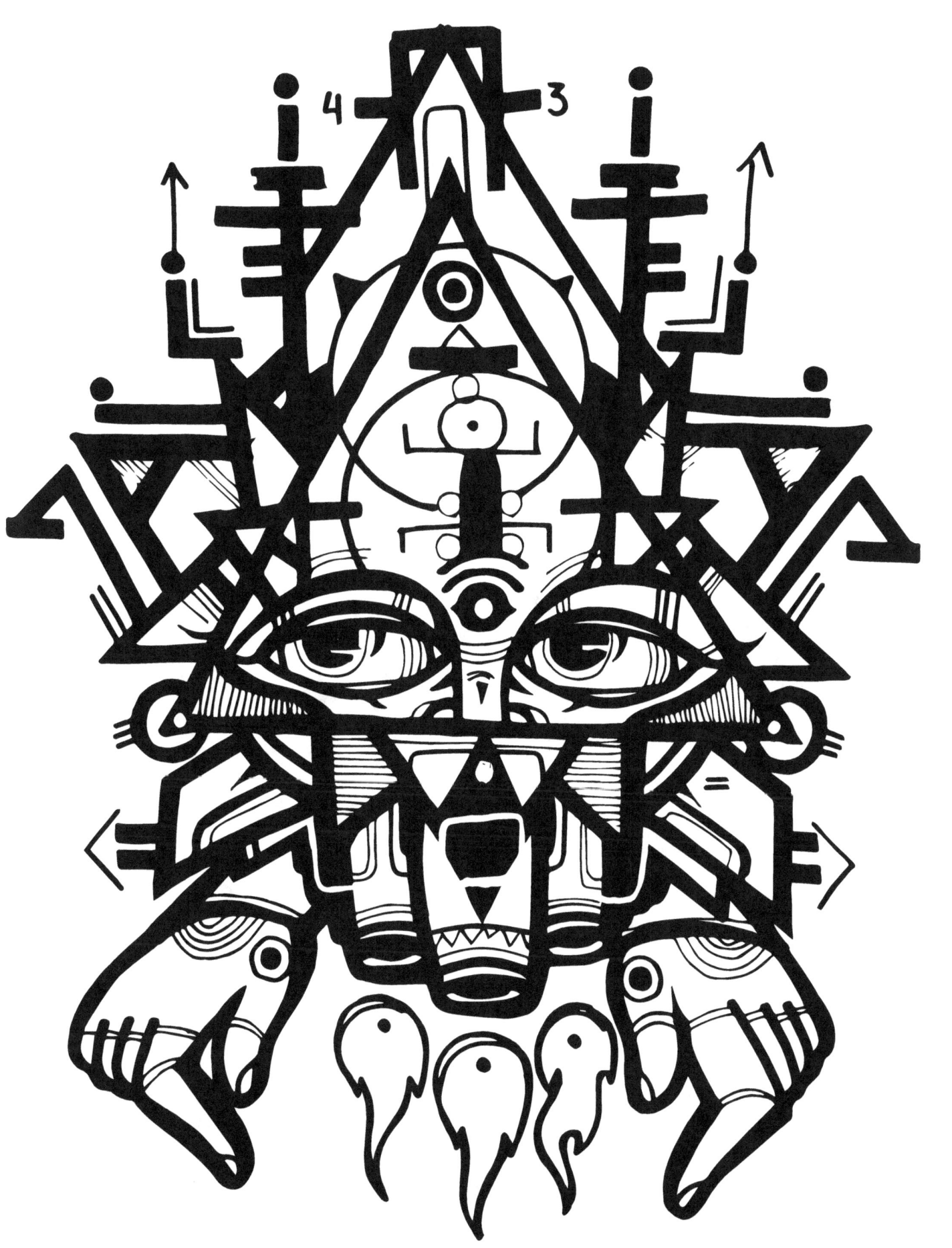

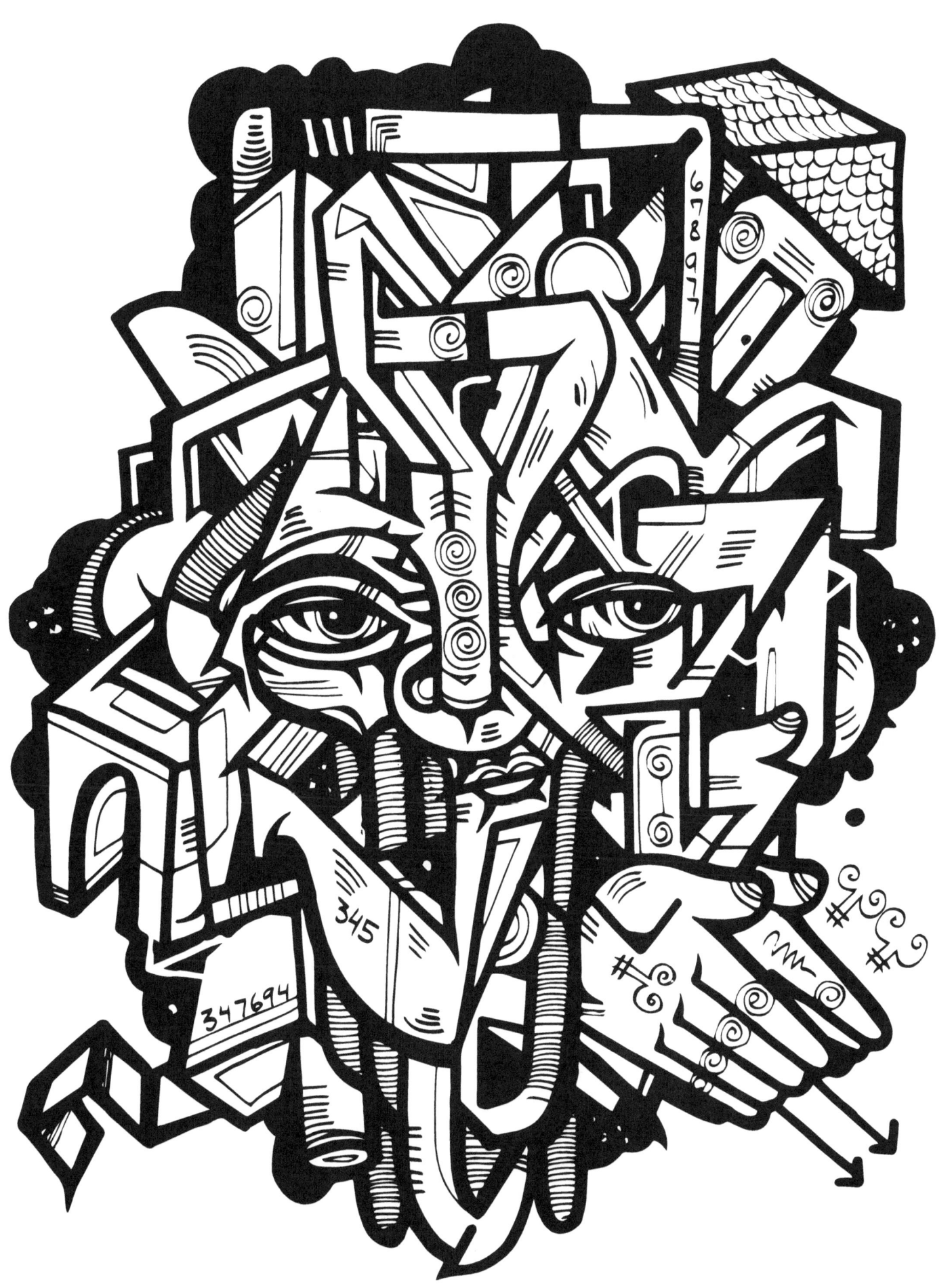

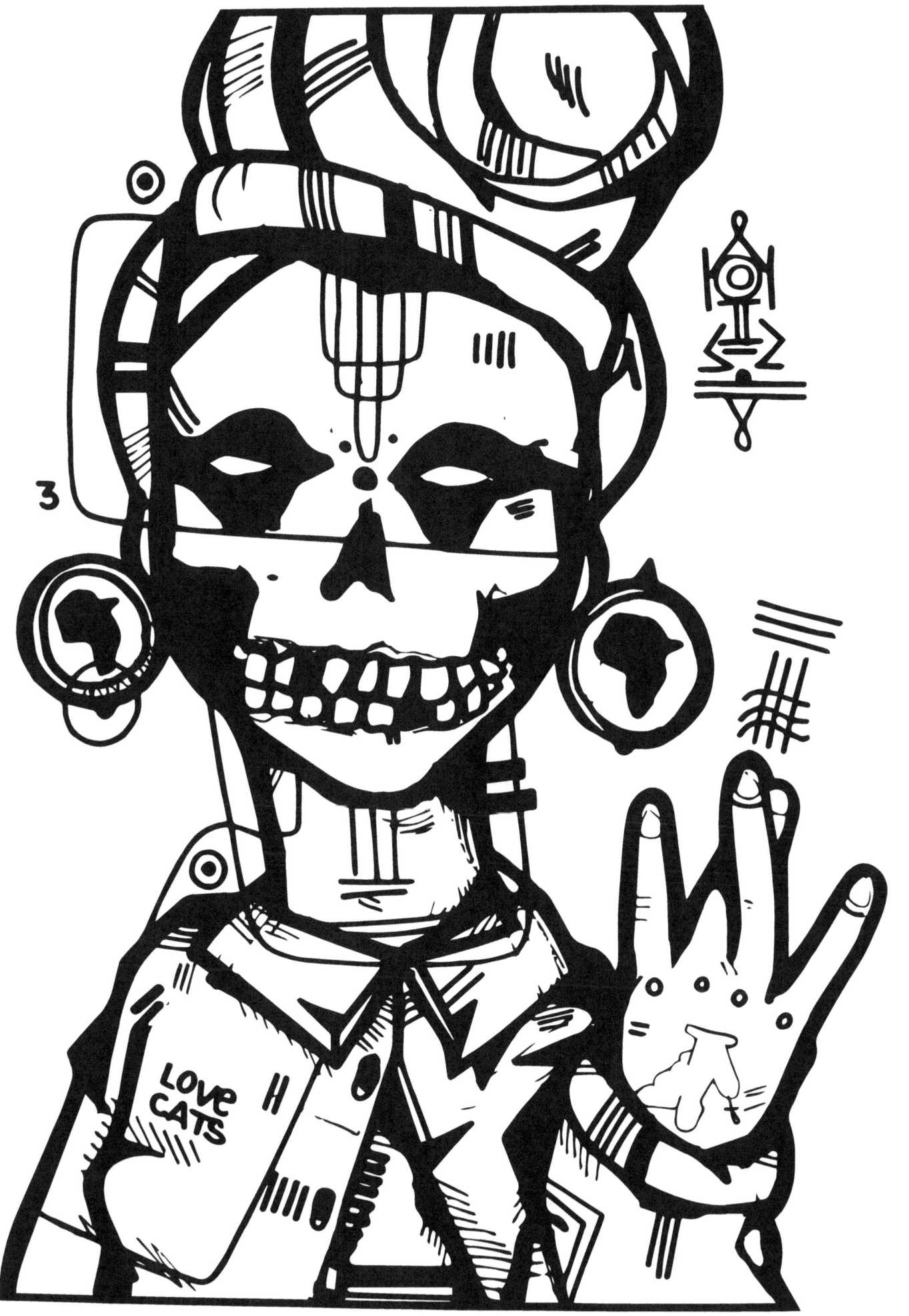

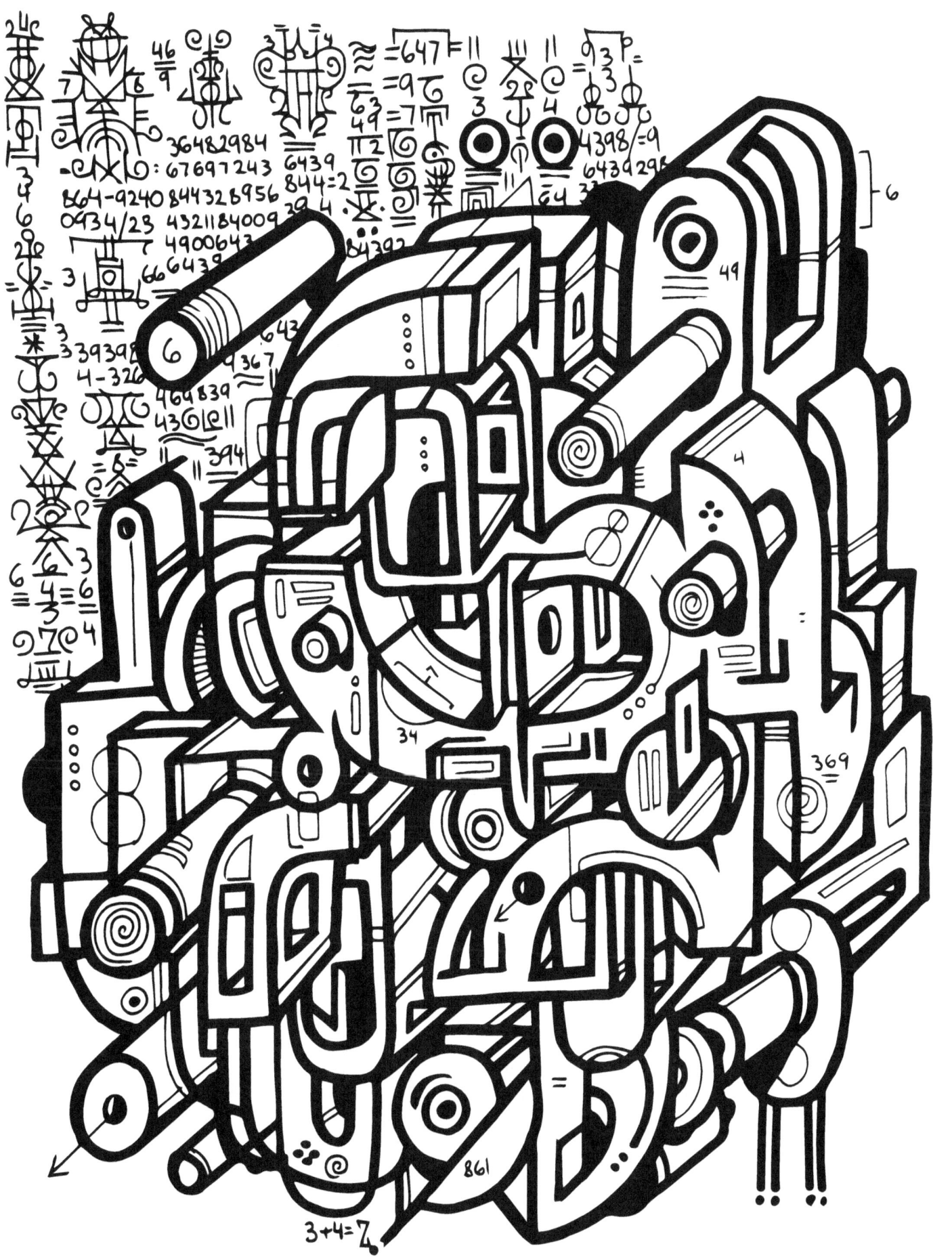

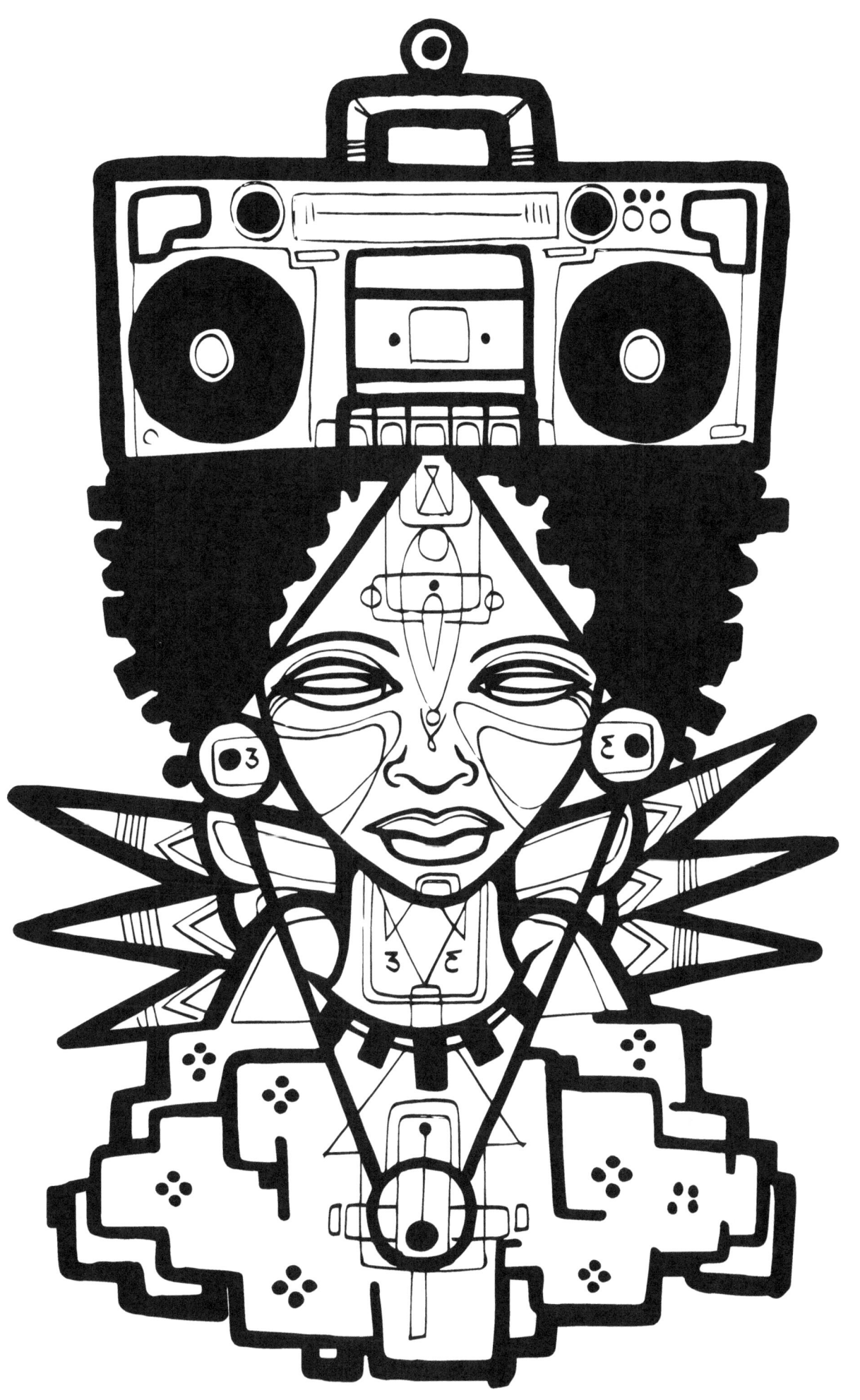

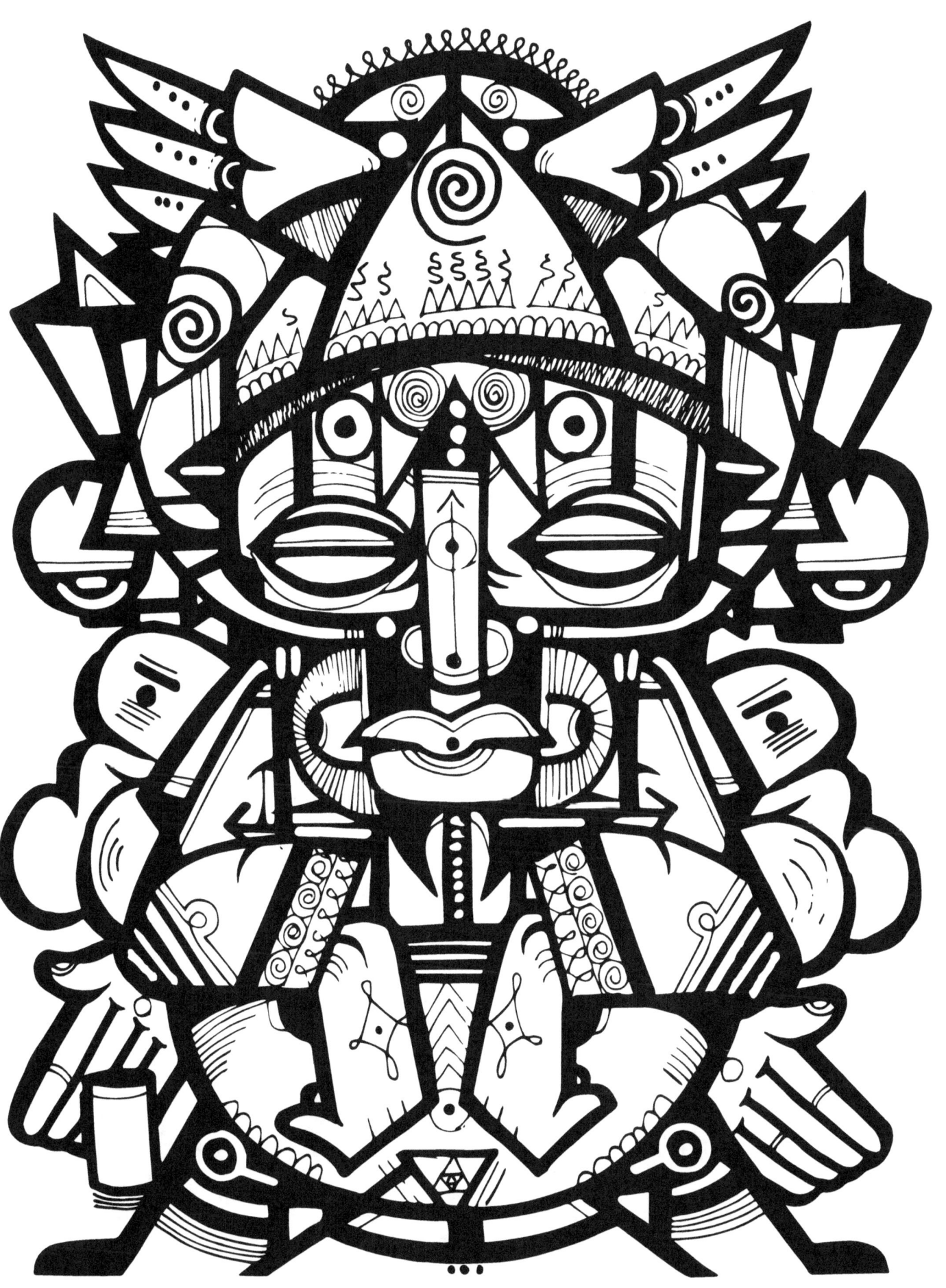